The All-Party Oireachtas Committee was established on 3 July 1996. Its terms of reference are:

In order to provide focus to the place and relevance of the Constitution and to establish those areas where Constitutional change may be desirable or necessary, the All-Party Committee will undertake a full review of the Constitution. In undertaking this review, the All-Party Committee will have regard to the following:

a   *the Report of the Constitution Review Group*

b   *certain constitutional matters, ie Articles 2 and 3, the Right to Bail, Cabinet Confidentiality and Votes for Emigrants which are the subject of separate consideration by the Government*

c   *participation in the All-Party Committee would involve no obligation to support any recommendations which might be made, even if made unanimously*

d   *members of the All-Party Committee, either as individuals or as Party representatives, would not be regarded as committed in any way to support such recommendations*

e   *members of the All-Party Committee shall keep their respective Party Leaders informed from time to time of the progress of the Committee's work*

f   *none of the parties, in Government or Opposition, would be precluded from dealing with matters within the All-Party Committee's terms of reference while it is sitting, and*

g   *whether there might be a single draft of non-controversial amendments to the Constitution to deal with technical matters.*

The committee comprises nine TDs and two senators:

> Austin Currie, TD, Minister of State
> Síle de Valera, TD
> Frances Fitzgerald, TD
> Senator Ann Gallagher
> Brian Lenihan, TD
> Kathleen Lynch, TD
> Derek McDowell, TD
> Michael McDowell, TD
> Willie O'Dea, TD
> Jim O'Keeffe, TD
> Senator Michael O'Kennedy.

The secretariat is provided by the Institute of Public Administration:

> Jim O'Donnell, *secretary*
> John Conlon, *assistant secretary*.

At its first meeting on 5 July 1996 the committee elected Jim O'Keeffe, TD, as chairman. At its second meeting on 25 July 1996 it elected Senator Michael O'Kennedy as vice-chairman.

While no constitutional issue is excluded from the committee's remit, it is not a body with exclusive concern for constitutional amendments: the Government, as the executive, is free to make constitutional proposals at any time; and indeed in November 1996 it successfully proposed that Article 40.4 be amended to allow changes in the legislation on bail. Moreover, any political party represented in the Dáil may also take a constitutional initiative at any time.

Contents

Jim O'Keeffe TD, chairman of the All-Party Oireachtas Committee on the Constitution

Foreword

The Constitution Review Group considered that the time available to it did not allow it to carry out a thorough analysis of all the issues relating to Seanad Éireann.

The All-Party Oireachtas Committee on the Constitution decided to get the task under way quickly. It commissioned a report, *Options for the Future of Seanad Éireann,* from John Coakley, Department of Politics, UCD and Professor Michael Laver, Department of Political Science, TCD, which was received by the Committee in December 1996. I wish to express the Committee's gratitude to the authors for the speed and care with which they produced the report. An original piece of research, it stimulated the Committee to produce with assuredness a fresh approach to the work of Seanad Éireann.

This second progress report represents, with the first progress report, the conclusions the Committee has reached to date.

Third Progress Report

In its next report the Committee will deal with the Presidency.

Jim O'Keeffe, TD
Chairman
April 1997

Seanad Éireann

Seanad Éireann

Articles 18, 19 – Seanad Éireann

18.1 Seanad Éireann shall be composed of sixty members, of whom eleven shall be nominated members and forty-nine shall be elected members.

18.2 A person to be eligible for membership of Seanad Éireann must be eligible to become a member of Dáil Éireann.

18.3 The nominated members of Seanad Éireann shall be nominated, with their prior consent, by the Taoiseach who is appointed next after the re-assembly of Dáil Éireann following the dissolution thereof which occasions the nomination of the said members.

18.4.1° The elected members of Seanad Éireann shall be elected as follows:-

i. Three shall be elected by the National University of Ireland.

ii. Three shall be elected by the University of Dublin.

iii. Forty-three shall be elected from panels of candidates constituted as hereinafter provided.

18.4.2° Provision may be made by law for the election, on a franchise and in the manner to be provided by law, by one or more of the following institutions, namely:

i. the universities mentioned in subsection 1° of this section,

ii. any other institutions of higher education in the State,

of so many members of Seanad Éireann as may be fixed by law in substitution for an equal number of the members to be elected pursuant to paragraphs i and ii of the said subsection 1°.

A member or members of Seanad Éireann may be elected under this

Although its report has some discussion on Seanad Éireann (see Appendix I), the Constitution Review Group considered that the time available to it did not allow it to carry out a thorough analysis of that house. It recommended therefore that 'a separate comprehensive, independent examination of all issues relating to Seanad Éireann' should be carried out.

The All-Party Oireachtas Committee on the Constitution decided to get this task under way quickly. It commissioned a report, *Options for the Future of Seanad Éireann,* from John Coakley, Department of Political Science, University College Dublin and Professor Michael Laver, Department of Political Science, Trinity College Dublin, which the authors presented to the committee on 5 December 1996 (see Appendix II). The committee also invited submissions from serving senators and a number of distinguished former senators. On 30 January 1997, the chairman opened a debate in the Seanad extending over two days on the composition and role of the Seanad. In addition, the committee received a number of submissions on the Seanad from the public (see page 114).

The Constitution Review Group observed:

> The rationale for having two houses of parliament in a unitary state is based on two important features of any mature democracy. The first is the need to take account of political interests that may not be adequately represented in the main house; the second is the need for some final review of legislative proposals before they become binding on all.

It concluded that if its recommended review 'does not resolve the issue of representation ... in a satisfactory manner, serious consideration will need to be given to the abolition of the Seanad and the transfer of its role and functions to other parts of the political system'.

background

Parliaments with two houses are the product of history rather than the architectural exuberance of politicians. As the Constitution Review Group puts it:

> Historically, parliament in Europe was a construct whereby, through negotiation, a king or queen shared the powers of state with those who could supply resources – with, at first, the big landowners (seigneurs or local lords and the Church represented by bishops and abbots) and subsequently with strong farmers and wealthy merchants (the commoners) too. Thus in Britain parliament evolved as a two-house (bicameral) assembly (a House of Lords and a House of Commons). In France it evolved as a three-house (tricameral) assembly – for aristocrats, clerics and the

subsection by institutions grouped together or by a single institution.

18.4.3° Nothing in this Article shall be invoked to prohibit the dissolution by law of a university mentioned in subsection 1° of this section.

18.5 Every election of the elected members of Seanad Éireann shall be held on the system of proportional representation by means of the single transferable vote, and by secret postal ballot.

18.6 The members of Seanad Éireann to be elected by the Universities shall be elected on a franchise and in the manner to be provided by law.

18.7.1° Before each general election of the members of Seanad Éireann to be elected from panels of candidates, five panels of candidates shall be formed in the manner provided by law containing respectively the names of persons having knowledge and practical experience of the following interests and services, namely:-

i. National Language and Culture, Literature, Art, Education and such professional interests as may be defined by law for the purpose of this panel;

ii. Agriculture and allied interests, and Fisheries;

iii. Labour, whether organised or unorganised;

iv. Industry and Commerce, including banking, finance, accountancy, engineering and architecture;

v. Public Administration and social services, including voluntary social activities.

18.7.2° Not more than eleven and, subject to the provisions of Article 19 hereof, not less than five members of Seanad Éireann shall be elected from any one panel.

18.8 A general election for Seanad Éireann shall take place not later than ninety days after a dissolution of Dáil Éireann, and the first meeting of Seanad Éireann after the general election

enfranchised common people respectively – until the French Revolution made France temporarily a unicameral state.

Initially the executive power of the state was wielded by the monarch who found it convenient that legislative and financial powers should be divided among the houses of parliament. That situation offered the monarch opportunities to influence and manipulate members of the houses, and to some extent neutralise the houses, by balancing one against the other. The supremacy of the monarch was symbolised by the power to veto legislation. In France, one of the jibes the revolutionaries threw at Louis XVI was 'Monsieur Veto'. In Irish historical experience, the repugnance with which George IV finally signed the Bill to emancipate Catholics was the epiphany of the eclipse of royal power.

Modern history has seen momentous shifts in the locus of the executive power of the state, as a result of a process of democratisation, first from the monarch to parliament, then to the democratic lower house of parliament and, finally, within parliament, from the lower house to its executive committee, the government. Broadly speaking, this process, which began in the nineteenth century, has seen many states replace their monarchs by a popularly elected or, as is more frequently the case, an indirectly elected president. Where monarchs have been retained, they play the role of ceremonial head of state, having relinquished virtually all executive powers. The process has also thrown into relief the non-democratic origins of upper houses and has led to a trend towards having unicameral legislatures. In 1967, the first All-Party Committee on the Constitution was able to say that in having a second chamber Ireland resembled 'most modern democracies'. The position today, however, is that only a quarter of the national parliaments of unitary states covered in the Inter-Parliamentary Union's database (forty out of one hundred and fifty-six) have second chambers. By a curious inversion, democratisation has also produced a problem for democracy: a government, once elected by the lower house, becomes the effective master of the people's representatives through the iron discipline of the party system and the standing orders of the house or houses of parliament.

Irish experience

In Ireland, the first national assembly since the Act of Union, Dáil Éireann, which met in January 1919, was a unicameral body. The national parliament established under the Constitution of the Irish Free State in 1922 – the Oireachtas – was a bicameral body consisting of the Dáil and the Senate. The nomination procedure for that Senate was designed to ensure representation for the Unionist minority in the south, and in fact the landed gentry and the ex-Unionist community were strongly and disproportionately represented in the first Senate. In 1936, the government abolished the Senate because it was blocking its legislative programme. However, Eamon de Valera's 1937 Constitution, *Bunreacht na hÉireann*, provided for a Senate – Seanad Éireann. The vocational system was presented as an apt means of bringing into the Seanad expertise and specialist knowledge. The arrangements for election of members, and the appointment of eleven of them by the Taoiseach, as well as the standing orders of both houses, however, ensure that the Seanad is largely the creature of the government and the Dáil.

shall take place on a day to be fixed by the President on the advice of the Taoiseach.

18.9 Every member of Seanad Éireann shall, unless he previously dies, resigns, or becomes disqualified, continue to hold office until the day before the polling day of the general election for Seanad Éireann next held after his election or nomination.

18.10.1° Subject to the foregoing provisions of this Article elections of the elected members of Seanad Éireann shall be regulated by law.

18.10.2° Casual vacancies in the number of the nominated members of Seanad Éireann shall be filled by nomination by the Taoiseach with the prior consent of persons so nominated.

18.10.3° Casual vacancies in the number of the elected members of Seanad Éireann shall be filled in the manner provided by law.

Article 19

Provision may be made by law for the direct election by any functional or vocational group or association or council of so many members of Seanad Éireann as may be fixed by such law in substitution for an equal number of the members to be elected from the corresponding panels of candidates constituted under Article 18 of this Constitution.

Article 20 – Legislation

20.1 Every Bill initiated in and passed by Dáil Éireann shall be sent to Seanad Éireann and may, unless it be a Money Bill, be amended in Seanad Éireann and Dáil Éireann shall consider any such amendment.

20.2.1° A Bill other than a Money Bill may be initiated in Seanad Éireann, and if passed by Seanad Éireann, shall be introduced in Dáil Éireann.

20.2.2° A Bill initiated in Seanad Éireann if amended in Dáil Éireann

Coakley/Laver provide a measure of the legislative activity of the Senate of the Irish Free State and Seanad Éireann:

> ... the Senate of the Irish Free State left a creditable legislative record. If this is measured in terms of amendments made to Bills, the raw figures are high. In all, amendments affected 37% of Bills during the life of the first Senate (1922-36), and eight Bills were rejected, of which two were subsequently dropped by the government. As a standard of comparison, during the lifetime of the Seanad (from 1938 to 19 September 1995) 18% of Bills were amended in the Seanad, but Bills were rejected outright on only one occasion. (Under existing constitutional arrangements, the disputed measure was subsequently passed.)

The relatively greater activity, measured in this way, of the Senate of the Irish Free State is not necessarily to be ascribed to the quality of the members of that house. The distinguished former senator, James Dooge, in his contribution to *Essays in Memory of Alexis Fitzgerald*, points out that the proportion of Bills amended by the first Senate decreased to a quarter as experience in legislative drafting was developed. Moreover, during the period of Seanad Éireann, a great number of Bills have been either simple in character or merely extensions of existing enactments – in contrast to the breaking of new ground during the period of the first Senate. Dooge further observes that in the case of a number of Bills of distinct political significance the number of Seanad amendments has been remarkably high. He also points out that study of the actual revision work of the Seanad provides numerous instances where amendments seeking certain effects which had been rejected in the partisan atmosphere of the Dáil were accepted by a minister after the more objective debate conducted in the Seanad. Moreover, in some cases where ministers are unwilling to amend a Bill in the Seanad, particularly if it comes late in the legislative season, because it would require returning to the Dáil for confirmation of the amendment, the outcome is not necessarily negative – the Seanad debates are noted by ministers and their advisers and amendments that are not accepted become in many cases the stuff of later legislation. (See Appendix III, 'Bills amended by the Seanad').

but should Seanad Éireann continue to exist?

Constitutionalists have long argued the issue whether there should be an upper house. The great constitutional lawyer of the French revolution, the Abbé Sieyès, was vehemently opposed: 'If a second chamber dissents from the first, it is mischievous; if it agrees, it is superfluous'. However, George Washington felt that an upper house was needed to act as a check on the lower house. To Thomas Jefferson, who once protested to him against the establishment of a two-house legislature, Washington posed the question, 'Why do you pour coffee into your saucer?' 'To cool it', replied Jefferson. 'Even so', said Washington, 'we pour legislation into the senatorial saucer to cool it'. The function of the upper house in providing calm deliberation and deep analysis of national issues is an important one. However, the idea of an upper house as a check on the supposed impetuosity of the people's representatives in the lower house seems to play to the ancient classical prejudice against democracy as readily degenerating to mob rule; and, of course, it seeks to accommodate the medieval reality that powerful people had a natural claim to a separate legislative say.

shall be considered as a Bill initiated in Dáil Éireann.

20.3 *A Bill passed by either House and accepted by the other House shall be deemed to have been passed by both Houses.*

Article 21 – Money Bills

21.1.1° *Money Bills shall be initiated in Dáil Éireann only.*

21.1.2° *Every Money Bill passed by Dáil Éireann shall be sent to Seanad Éireann for its recommendations.*

21.2.1° *Every Money Bill sent to Seanad Éireann for its recommendations shall, at the expiration of a period not longer than twenty-one days after it shall have been sent to Seanad Éireann, be returned to Dáil Éireann, which may accept or reject all or any of the recommendations of Seanad Éireann.*

21.2.2° *If such Money Bill is not returned by Seanad Éireann to Dáil Éireann within such twenty-one days or is returned within such twenty-one days with recommendations which Dáil Éireann does not accept, it shall be deemed to have been passed by both Houses at the expiration of the said twenty-one days.*

Article 22.2.2° – 6°

22.2.2° *Seanad Éireann, by a resolution, passed at a sitting at which not less than thirty members are present, may request the President to refer the question whether the Bill is or is not a Money Bill to a Committee of Privileges.*

22.2.3° *If the President after consultation with the Council of State decides to accede to the request he shall appoint a Committee of Privileges consisting of an equal number of members of Dáil Éireann and of Seanad Éireann and a Chairman who shall be a Judge of the Supreme Court: these appointments shall be made after consultation with the Council of State. In the case of an equality of votes but not otherwise the Chairman shall be entitled to vote.*

It is true that a strong rationale can be presented for having a second chamber in a federal state, as in the United States, where the lower house is filled by a popular vote with members from each state in proportion to the size of its population and the upper house is filled by two popularly elected senators from each state, and where separate legislative powers are assigned to each house. In a unitary state it is difficult to fill the second house with popularly returned members without institutionalising the probability of clashes between the two houses, perhaps leading to legislative deadlock, because of their equal legitimacy in terms of popular mandate and the impossibility of offering them different areas of legislative predominance without raising the question: why have two houses? Of the forty unitary states with two chambers dealt with in Coakley/Laver, only eleven return second chambers filled completely on the basis of a popular vote. Most of the second chambers are filled by indirect elections or ex officio or by appointment (see Appendix II). Being demonstrably less democratically based than the lower house, the upper house in most unitary bicameral states is given less powers (see Appendix II), as in Ireland.

The Committee is persuaded by the argument in Coakley/Laver that the Seanad does make a useful contribution to the democratic life of the state. The savings achieved if it were abolished – it costs about £2.8 million per annum to run – could be illusory because some of the functions it carries out would need to be reallocated to other parts of the political system. Furthermore, there would be a serious loss to the Dáil because the disappearance of senators would make the task of manning the committee system extremely difficult. The Committee also agrees with Coakley/Laver that the Seanad is a resource that could be deployed to far greater effect if it were reformed.

Coakley/Laver present with great clarity the whole range of options available from international experience as to the powers Seanad Éireann might be given. The Committee has been struck by two factors in particular: the trend in unitary states to have unicameral legislatures and the reality of Irish politics that the Seanad is not allowed to proceed in any way that would allow it to frustrate the wishes of the Dáil. From this it concludes that reform of the Seanad should not move in the direction of giving it more powers – something that congrues with the views expressed by a number of senators in the recent debate in Seanad Éireann.

Moreover, whatever about the past, the modern reality is that, typically, legislation is now prepared within government departments. A sponsoring minister has available the knowledge, skill and experience of his or her civil servants, the officials in the state-sponsored bodies attached to his or her department and officials from other relevant areas of the public service, such as local authorities and health boards, the reports of research bodies, input from the institutions of the European Union, and consultations with interest groups either singly or grouped within such organisations as the National Economic and Social Forum (NESF). This process makes for broad consensus before Bills reach the Dáil.

So it is the Dáil which now provides the check on the promoters of legislation – the government. In the Dáil the government's proposals are paraded in public and they must win approval as being in the public interest. This means that the government's supporters in the house

22.2.4° *The President shall refer the question to the Committee of Privileges so appointed and the Committee shall report its decision thereon to the President within twenty-one days after the day on which the Bill was sent to Seanad Éireann.*

22.2.5° *The decision of the Committee shall be final and conclusive.*

22.2.6° *If the President after consultation with the Council of State decides not to accede to the request of Seanad Éireann, or if the Committee of Privileges fails to report within the time hereinbefore specified the certificate of the Chairman of Dáil Éireann shall stand confirmed.*

Articles 23, 24 – Time for Consideration of Bills

23.1 *This Article applies to every Bill passed by Dáil Éireann and sent to Seanad Éireann other than a Money Bill or a Bill the time for the consideration of which by Seanad Éireann shall have been abridged under Article 24 of this Constitution.*

23.1.1° *Whenever a Bill to which this Article applies is within the stated period defined in the next following sub-section either rejected by Seanad Éireann or passed by Seanad Éireann with amendments to which Dáil Éireann does not agree or is neither passed (with or without amendment) nor rejected by Seanad Éireann within the stated period, the Bill shall, if Dáil Éireann so resolves within one hundred and eighty days after the expiration of the stated period be deemed to have been passed by both House of the Oireachtas on the day on which the resolution is passed.*

23.1.2° *The stated period is the period of ninety days commencing on the day on which the Bill is first sent by Dáil Éireann to Seanad Éireann or any longer period agreed upon in respect of the Bill by both Houses of the Oireachtas.*

23.2.1° *The preceding section of this Article shall apply to a Bill which is initiated in and passed*

must feel that the proposals can be credibly presented to their constituents as being socially beneficial and that any serious criticisms made by the opposition have been either rebutted or taken into account by amendments. If a government were simply to rely on its arithmetical superiority and party discipline to impose its will brutally on the Dáil, it would run the risk of winning legislative battles but losing the political war that follows the dissolution of the Dáil and ends in the formation of a new government. This reality means that as much resources as possible must be placed at the service of the Dáil.

Seanad Éireann should be a consultative body where people with knowledge, experience and judgment over the whole spectrum of public affairs should be available in a broadly non-partisan way to help the Dáil to carry out its function more effectively and more efficiently.

Having arrived at this conclusion the Committee finds itself in a position to take a fresh overall view of what the Seanad should do and what its composition should be.

Functions

1   general

The essential function that Dáil Éireann carries out is to test the proposals coming from the government to see whether they are really in the public interest. It is often notoriously difficult to determine what exactly the public interest is, *pace* the legendary citizen who invariably found it easy: 'When I want to know if a proposal is in the public interest I ask myself: how will it affect *me*?' We all have a capacity to present our own interests in highly acceptable social terms but the adversarial character of the Dáil debates exposes the real intent of legislative proposals. This analytical process, being confrontational and often sharply focused on the short-term aspect of issues, attracts the attention of the media. As a result, Dáil debates sometimes have, for the public, a destructive character. However, the analytical phase is followed by a creative, synthetical phase in which proposals are re-shaped and amendments made before the Bills are passed. In this phase it is essential to the quality of legislation that it should be considered in medium and long-term perspectives. It is difficult for deputies, given the complexity and variety of Bills and the multifarious calls upon their time, to develop and sustain such medium and long-term perspectives. This is a systems weakness that needs to be addressed. The Committee believes that the Seanad could provide a means of doing that.

A major concern of Seanad Éireann should be to develop and sustain medium and long-term perspectives across the spectrum of government policy areas.

Even casual observation of the Irish political system reveals that there is marked gender imbalance among public representatives. This is another systems weakness because it means that the knowledge, experience and sensibility of women are largely absent from the processes through which the state seeks to express the values of its people. The Committee believes that reform of the Seanad provides an opportunity to redress this imbalance significantly in the short term by prescribing a substantial number of women senators. By giving greater

by Seanad Éireann, amended by Dáil Éireann, and accordingly deemed to have been initiated in Dáil Éireann.

23.2.2° *For the purpose of this application the stated period shall in relation to such a Bill commence on the day on which the Bill is first sent to Seanad Éireann after having been amended by Dáil Éireann.*

Article 24

24.1 *If and whenever on the passage by Dáil Éireann of any Bill, other than a Bill expressed to be a Bill containing a proposal to amend the Constitution, the Taoiseach certifies by messages in writing addressed to the President and to the Chairman of each House of the Oireachtas that, in the opinion of the Government, the Bill is urgent and immediately necessary for the preservation of the public peace and security, or by reason of the existence of a public emergency, whether domestic or international, the time for the consideration of such Bill by Seanad Éireann shall, if Dáil Éireann so resolves and if the President, after consultation with the Council of State, concurs, be abridged to such period as shall be specified in the resolution.*

24.2 *Where a Bill, the time for the consideration of which by Seanad Éireann has been abridged under this Article,*

(a) is, in the case of a Bill which is not a Money Bill, rejected by Seanad Éireann or passed by Seanad Éireann with amendments to which Dáil Éireann does not agree or neither passed nor rejected by Seanad Éireann, or

(b) is, in the case of a Money Bill, either returned by Seanad Éireann to Dáil Éireann with recommendations which Dáil Éireann does not accept or is not returned by Seanad Éireann to Dáil Éireann,

within the period specified in the resolution, the Bill shall be deemed to have been passed by both Houses of the Oireachtas at the expiration of that period.

numbers of women experience of political life and increased scope to distinguish themselves in the media and other public fora, the measure would lead to markedly greater participation by women in the Dáil and in the European Parliament in the middle and long term.

The nomination, electoral and appointment procedures for senators should aim to produce gender balance in the Seanad.

2 specific

The two specific functions carried out by the Dáil are to debate and vote on legislative proposals and to review the activities of the government.

a) legislation

i) *Irish legislation* In managing its legislative programme, the government is inclined to view both houses of the Oireachtas as hazards through which it must run legislation. Its major focus is on the Dáil because the Dáil has real capacity to effect changes in legislation. It therefore introduces nearly all legislation there. Because it usually commands a majority in the Seanad, and because the Seanad has essentially an advisory function to the Dáil, the government tends to view the passage of legislation through the Seanad as a formal process that can be speeded up at will. Since the Seanad's legislative work is, in the main, residual to that of the Dáil, it does not come in a smooth flow but in sporadic rushes. The Seanad's standing orders allow it to conduct debates on major reports and issues of national concern and so it can devote itself to matters ostensibly of importance when it is awaiting legislative work from the Dáil. However, when such debates are not directly inspired by the government – and that is often the case – they present as hortatory exercises. Nonetheless, the value of the legislative work that is done by the Seanad is acknowledged by the Dáil and should be continued. But it should be managed differently.

The Committee believes that the legislative function of the Dáil could be greatly improved if legislation were either:

> introduced in the Seanad, brought through its first three stages, sent to the Dáil with the Seanad's observations and taken from a third stage in the Dáil to final decision

> or

> having been introduced in the Dáil and taken to its third stage there, sent to the Seanad for its observations, returned to the Dáil, and brought to decision there.

The facility should remain with the government of expediting urgent legislation through the Dáil with only formal reference to the Seanad.

ii) *EU legislation* Ireland's membership of the EU has created a broad bridge over which a huge volume of EU regulations, directives, decisions, recommendations and opinions is carried. This traffic represents how the powers ceded by the member states under the Treaties are being used. It is clear that careful checks on

24.3 When a Bill the time for the consideration of which by Seanad Éireann has been abridged under this Article becomes law it shall remain in force for a period of ninety days from the date of its enactment and no longer unless, before the expiration of that period, both Houses shall have agreed that such law shall remain in force for a longer period and the longer period so agreed upon shall have been specified in resolutions passed by both Houses.

Article 27 – Reference of Bills to the People

27 This Article applies to any Bill, other than a Bill expressed to be a Bill containing a proposal for the amendment of this Constitution, which shall have been deemed, by virtue of Article 23 hereof, to have been passed by both Houses of the Oireachtas.

27.1 A majority of the members of Seanad Éireann and not less than one-third of the members of Dáil Éireann may by a joint petition addressed to the President by them under this Article request the President to decline to sign and promulgate as a law any Bill to which this Article applies on the ground that the Bill contains a proposal of such national importance that the will of the people thereon ought to be ascertained.

27.2 Every such petition shall be in writing and shall be signed by the petitioners whose signatures shall be verified in the manner prescribed by law.

27.3 Every such petition shall contain a statement of the particular ground or grounds on which the request is based, and shall be presented to the President not later than four days after the date on which the Bill shall have been deemed to have been passed by both Houses of the Oireachtas.

27.4.1° Upon receipt of a petition addressed to him under this Article, the President shall forthwith consider such petition and shall, after consultation with the Council of State, pronounce his decision thereon not later than

it should be carried out by the Oireachtas. Owing to the heavy calls upon their time Dáil deputies find themselves unable to do this effectively.

The Committee believes that the Seanad could play a major role in ensuring that this important task is carried out. Provision could be made to have MEPs take part in debates in the house, although without voting rights. Relevant EU commissioners and senior commission officials could be invited to the house for discussions on the EU's legislative programme and the Seanad should monitor EU regulations and directives and produce reports for the Dáil on the impact of, and trends in, that legislation. It seems to the Committee that, if the Seanad tackled such a task with imagination, energy and high critical power, it could convey to the people in clear realistic terms what the European dimension adds to our lives and offer sound advice on how the state should seek to shape EU policies.

iii) *Statutory instruments* These are specific regulations made by ministers under general powers granted to them by an Act. They have the effect of laws and the Oireachtas should keep a check on them. Again Dáil deputies, owing to the heavy calls upon their time, find themselves unable to do this effectively.

The Committee believes that the Seanad could carry out this important task by drawing up reports on statutory instruments for the Dáil.

b) *review*

i) *Government activities* The public service is an immense, variegated and traditionally secretive cluster of organisations which the Dáil can only partially review through parliamentary questions to individual ministers and through the investigations of such committees as the Public Accounts Committee. The Seanad helps the Dáil in this work by participating in joint committees.

The Committee believes that the Seanad could help the Dáil further by carrying out special reviews of government programmes assigned to it by the Dáil.

ii) *Policy reports* Major policy reports on their publication excite short-term interest in the media.

Such reports should be debated by the Seanad in such a way that the medium and long-term perspectives are developed and sustained which would provide the proper intellectual context for the critical appraisal by the Dáil of the policies contained in Bills.

iii) *Northern Ireland* There is a need to maintain a focus on relationships with Northern Ireland in terms of both all-Ireland and EU initiatives in such areas as the promotion of tourism and cross-border trade.

ten days after the date on which the Bill to which such petition relates shall have been deemed to have been passed by both Houses of the Oireachtas.

27.4.2° If the Bill or any provision thereof is or has been referred to the Supreme Court under Article 26 of this Constitution, it shall not be obligatory on the President to consider the petition unless or until the Supreme Court has pronounced a decision on such reference to the effect that the said Bill or the said provision thereof is not repugnant to this Constitution or to any provision thereof, and, if a decision to that effect is pronounced by the Supreme Court, it shall not be obligatory on the President to pronounce his decision on the petition before the expiration of six days after the day on which the decision of the Supreme Court to the effect aforesaid is pronounced.

27.5.1° In every case in which the President decides that a Bill the subject of a petition under this Article contains a proposal of such national importance that the will of the people thereon ought to be ascertained, he shall inform the Taoiseach and the Chairman of each House of the Oireachtas accordingly in writing under his hand and Seal and shall decline to sign and promulgate such Bill as a law unless and until the proposal shall have been approved either

i. by the people at a Referendum in accordance with the provisions of section 2 of Article 47 of this Constitution within a period of eighteen months from the date of the President's decision, or

ii. by a resolution of Dáil Éireann passed within the said period after a dissolution and re-assembly of Dáil Éireann.

27.5.2° Whenever a proposal contained in a Bill the subject of a petition under this Article shall have been approved either by the people or by a resolution of Dáil Éireann in accordance with the foregoing provisions of this section, such Bill shall as soon as may be after such approval be

The Committee believes that the presence in the Seanad of members from Northern Ireland would enhance the quality of communication and understanding. As with its treatment of EU legislation, the Seanad might usefully hear representatives of relevant interest groups from both north and south.

Composition

Reflection on the general and specific functions that need to be carried out suggests that the Seanad should be filled by people, as many as half of whom might be women, of proven good judgment and who collectively have knowledge and experience of politics, economics, and social and cultural affairs. In addition, experience of the Seanad as it exists suggests that the representatives of third-level institutions make an exceptional contribution and that former senior members of the Dáil who become senators (see Appendix III) bring a political realism to the work of the Seanad which it might otherwise lack.

Since the proposed role of the Seanad as a consultative resource to the Dáil is non-partisan, it is critically important to ensure that the requisite kinds of candidates are nominated and elected. Nonetheless the functions are political ones and the people and their representatives should be involved in the election or selection of members. To bring the Seanad closer to the people the Committee feels a number of members should be returned by direct elections; that another tranche of members should be indirectly elected; that the Taoiseach for particular reasons should continue to have the power to select a certain number of members; and that third-level institutions should continue to be drawn on by the election of a number of their graduates by the graduates of those institutions.

The current total membership of Seanad Éireann is sixty with forty-three members indirectly elected from panels (Article 18.4.1°iii), six from two university constituencies (Article 18.4.1°i and ii) and eleven nominated by the Taoiseach (Article 18.3). To carry out the functions now proposed for the Seanad the Committee recommends that the total membership of the Seanad should remain at sixty but should be derived as follows:

directly elected members (15)

One of the criticisms levelled at the Dáil is that issues raised often have a localist character. The fact that some 89% of Dáil deputies serve, or have served, on local authorities and that political loyalty, to some degree, is maintained through a local clientelist system makes it perhaps inevitable that this should be so. The Committee feels that the Seanad should be used to engage people who would be freer to take broader national or regional perspectives. For that reason it recommends that fifteen members should be returned from the European Parliament constituencies by the national electorate on the same day as the general elections. The Committee believes that this schema would encourage the nomination of people who have contributed significantly to various aspects of our society. It could also provide a proving ground for aspirant MEPs.

presented to the President for his signature and promulgation by him as a law and the President shall thereupon sign the Bill and duly promulgate it as a law.

27.6 In every case in which the President decides that a Bill the subject of a petition under this Article does not contain a proposal of such national importance that the will of the people thereon ought to be ascertained, he shall inform the Taoiseach and the Chairman of each House of the Oireachtas accordingly in writing under his hand and Seal, and such Bill shall be signed by the President not later than eleven days after the date on which the Bill shall have been deemed to have been passed by both Houses of the Oireachtas and shall be duly promulgated by him as a law.

Articles 28.7 – 8

28.7.1° The Taoiseach, the Tánaiste and the member of the Government who is in charge of the Department of Finance must be members of Dáil Éireann.

28.7.2° The other members of the Government must be members of Dáil Éireann or Seanad Éireann, but not more than two may be members of Seanad Éireann.

28.8 Every member of the Government shall have the right to attend and be heard in each House of the Oireachtas.

Article 31.2 i

31.2 The Council of State shall consist of the following members:

i. As ex-officio members: the Taoiseach, the Tánaiste, the Chief Justice, the President of the High Court, the Chairman of Dáil Éireann, the Chairman of Seanad Éireann, and the Attorney General.

Article 33.5

33.5.1° The Comptroller and Auditor General shall not be removed from office except for stated misbehaviour or incapacity, and then only upon resolutions passed by Dáil Éireann and by

indirectly elected members (28)

As Coakley/Laver point out, indirect election, that is to say, election by an electorate consisting of people who have been themselves elected by the people, is a common method of filling seats in an upper house. At present forty-three senators are indirectly elected from five panels. The Committee recommends that there should be twenty-eight indirectly elected members.

Fourteen should be elected by the incoming Dáil. This would provide opportunities for young, aspirant politicians and also facilitate the election of former members of the Dáil who might wish to continue to be involved in national affairs. Fourteen should be elected by the members of the county councils and county borough councils. This would engage local authority members who could bring their particular experience to national politics.

In order to address the systems weakness already mentioned of the marked gender imbalance among public representatives the Committee recommends that these elections should be carried out on the basis of two sub-panels, one for men and one for women with an equal number elected from each. The nomination and other electoral procedures should be left to legislation.

university/third level representation (6)

The Committee believes that six seats should continue to be allocated to third-level representatives. It accepts that there is a general perception that the present allocation of three seats to the National University of Ireland and three seats to the University of Dublin is unacceptable. It recommends that all Irish graduates of the institutions that fall within the remit of the Higher Education Authority and the National Council for Educational Awards should form the electorate for the six seats. The members should be returned from six single-seat constituencies each centred on a major institution:

- University College Dublin third-level constituency

- Trinity College Dublin third-level constituency

- the Leinster third-level constituency centred on Dublin City University and encompassing St Patrick's College Maynooth, Carlow Regional Technical College and the other Leinster third-level institutions

- the Connaught-Ulster third-level constituency centred on University College Galway and encompassing Letterkenny Regional Technical College and the other Connaught-Ulster third-level institutions

- the Mid-West third-level constituency centred on the University of Limerick and encompassing Limerick Regional Technical College and Tralee Regional Technical College

- the South-Munster third-level constituency centred on University College Cork and encompassing Cork Regional Technical College and the other South-Munster third-level institutions

Seanad Éireann calling for his removal.

33.5.2° *The Taoiseach shall duly notify the President of any such resolutions as aforesaid passed by Dáil Éireann and by Seanad Éireann and shall send him a copy of each such resolution certified by the Chairman of the House of the Oireachtas by which it shall have been passed.*

33.5.3° *Upon receipt of such notification and of copies of such resolutions, the President shall forthwith, by an order under his hand and Seal, remove the Comptroller and Auditor General from office.*

Article 35.4

35.4.1° *A judge of the Supreme Court or the High Court shall not be removed from office except for stated misbehaviour or incapacity, and then only upon resolutions passed by Dáil Éireann and by Seanad Éireann calling for his removal.*

35.4.2° *The Taoiseach shall duly notify the President of any such resolutions passed by Dáil Éireann and by Seanad Éireann, and shall send him a copy of every such resolution certified by the Chairman of the House of the Oireachtas by which it shall have been passed.*

35.4.3° *Upon receipt of such notification and of copies of such resolutions, the President shall forthwith, by an order under his hand and Seal, remove from office the judge to whom they relate.*

Legislation should provide for the determination of constituencies and the placing of graduates in them.

Taoiseach's nominees (11)

The Taoiseach should retain the power of appointing eleven senators, although not out of a concern that the government should have a majority in the Seanad but rather that it should have protagonists for its legislative programme there. The Committee recommends that three of the Taoiseach's eleven nominees should be representative of the various traditions in the North. It also recommends that the Taoiseach should maintain gender balance in his or her appointments within 40% – 60% limits.

Conclusion

Some of the above arrangements can be made by legislation under the existing provisions of the Constitution. However, constitutional amendments are required to provide for:

- the direct election of fifteen members
- the indirect election of twenty-eight members
- the election of six members from single-seat third-level constituencies.

This will require amendments to Article 18 sections 4 to 8.

Appendices

Appendix I

Seanad Éireann

Extract from the *Report of the Constitution Review Group*

INTRODUCTION

Historically, parliament in Europe was a construct whereby, through negotiation, a king or queen shared the powers of state with those who could supply resources – with, at first, the big landowners (seigneurs or local lords and the Church represented by bishops and abbots) and subsequently with strong farmers and wealthy merchants (the commoners) too. Thus in Britain parliament evolved as a two-house (bicameral) assembly (a House of Lords and a House of Commons). In France it evolved as a three-house (tricameral) assembly – for aristocrats, clerics and the enfranchised common people respectively – until the French Revolution made France temporarily a unicameral state.

Broadly speaking, in Britain, during the course of the nineteenth century and early twentieth century, the process of democratisation resulted in the transfer of the control of the executive powers of the state from the monarch to the Houses of Parliament, and in time mainly to the directly elected House of Commons.

In the United States of America a federal (rather than a unitary) form of government was established with substantive powers being shared between a House of Representatives (a body directly elected by the people, with each state returning a number of representatives broadly proportional to its population) and a Senate which represented the interests of the states and comprised two representatives from each state. The name Senate, with its connotations of age and experience, derives from the name of the ruling body of the ancient Roman Republic from which the American and French revolutionaries drew inspiration.

While all federal states have two houses, this is not true of all unitary states. For instance, in Europe, Ireland, Britain, France, Italy, the Czech Republic, Poland, Romania, Slovenia and Spain have upper houses but Bulgaria, Denmark, Estonia, Finland, Hungary, Iceland, Portugal, Norway, Latvia, Lithuania, the Slovak Republic and Sweden do not. However, where there is no second house there is normally provision for a second review of legislation before enactment. Thus, Luxembourg has a Council of State that fulfils some of the functions of an upper house. In Finland and Portugal, the house has a large and important committee that functions in some respects as a second chamber.

The national assembly which met in the Mansion House in January 1919 was a unicameral body – Dáil Éireann. The 1922 Saorstát Éireann Constitution provided for a Senate. Half of the members of that body were nominated by the head of government, half were elected by the Dáil. The nomination procedure was intended to ensure representation for the Unionist minority. A change in 1928 resulted in Senators being elected by the Oireachtas from a panel nominated by them. In time, the balance of political representation in the Dáil and Senate diverged and conflict between the Senate and the Government led to the abolition of the Senate in 1936.

In June 1936 the Second House of the Oireachtas Commission was appointed under the chairmanship of Chief Justice Aodh Ó Cinnéidigh. The commission's report indicated an extraordinary diversity of opinion on such questions as the composition and functions of a possible Seanad, and the most suitable electorate.

The publication of the Seanad Electoral (Parliamentary Members) Bill 1937, to implement the constitutional provision on the new Seanad, was referred to a special committee of fifteen deputies. After some inconclusive discussion of different methods of election for the Seanad, the committee decided that no useful purpose would be served by prolonging their deliberation and reported accordingly.

The 1937 Constitution also provided for two houses but represented a new approach. Seanad Éireann is now composed of sixty members, of whom eleven are nominated by the Taoiseach, six are elected by the graduates of two universities, and the remaining forty-three are elected from five panels representing aspects of national life (National Language and Culture, Agriculture, Labour, Industry and Commerce and Public Administration). Thus, the Constitution provides for the panel, or type of organisation, from which candidates are nominated. The method of constituting the panels, and the system of election, are governed by legislation. For the panel election, the electorate is very limited, consisting of Dáil Deputies, the outgoing Senators and members of county councils and county boroughs – a total of 965 in the 1993 election.

Apart from prescribing PR-STV as the voting process, the Constitution requires (Article 18.7) that there be five panels and that 'no more than eleven and ... not less than five members of Seanad Éireann shall be elected from any one panel'. The method of establishing the candidate list is otherwise left to statute. It follows that certain aspects of both panels and electorate could be changed by legislation without amendment of the Constitution.

Under Article 28.4.1° the Government is responsible to Dáil Éireann. The Seanad is a deliberative body with limited powers of initiation and review of legislation but with the capacity to initiate discussions on matters of public interest. A Money Bill may not be initiated in the Seanad, nor may the Seanad hold such a Bill for longer than twenty-one days before returning it to the Dáil, which can reject recommendations of the Seanad regarding such a Bill, as it can amendments proposed by the Seanad to ordinary Bills. Under Article 15, Senators have the same privileges and immunities as members of the Dáil. The Seanad also has power under Article 27, in combination with not less than one-third of the members of the Dáil, to request the President not to sign a Bill 'on the ground that the Bill contains a proposal of such national importance that the will of the people thereon ought to be ascertained'. This power has never been used.

The rationale for having two houses of parliament in a unitary state is based on two important features of any mature democracy. The first is the need to take account of political interests that may not be adequately represented in the main house; the second is the need for some final review of legislative proposals before they become binding on all. The so-called lower house is the primary legislature, representing the people generally and making or breaking governments. The primary purpose of an upper house is to provide a system of checks and balances on the legislative process. This can be done with more assurance if the composition of the upper house does not simply mirror that of the lower house.

The role and functions of the Seanad must be considered in relation to Ireland's cabinet system of government, which gives executive power to a Government appointed almost exclusively from members of Dáil Éireann and accountable to the people through their representatives in that house. This position is reflected in constitutional provisions which set out a system of governance that gives primacy to the relationship between the Government and the Dáil. At the same time, the Seanad tends to have the advantage over the Dáil of being a less hurried forum for discussion of the issues facing Irish society and the implications of legislative proposals. Members of the Seanad can bring their experience, knowledge and skills to bear on such matters with beneficial effect.

Disquiet has been expressed from time to time about the composition and functioning of the Seanad. In 1958, a Seanad Electoral Law Commission, chaired by Circuit Court Judge Joseph McCarthy, with nineteen other members, considered whether these shortcomings could be remedied within the terms of Articles 18 and 19, but came to no firm conclusions after deliberations lasting nine months. The deliberations of this commission covered the question of direct elections to the Seanad under Article 19. It received representations from more than thirty different trade or vocational organisations. The subject of whether or not a second house was necessary and, if so, how it should be constituted, was also considered inconclusively by the Committee on the Constitution (1967) (Report, paras 64-86). More recently, criticisms of the Seanad have centred on the duplication of representation as between the Dáil and the Seanad as well as on the question of its relevance to the modern political system. Few items of legislation originate there, although recently the percentage of more technical legislation originating with the Seanad has increased. Senators have been appointed as members of the Government on only two occasions. Senators cannot raise parliamentary questions and sittings of the Seanad are determined largely by the need to consider Bills passed by the Dáil. The electorate – members of the Oireachtas and councillors – means that party politics affect both the nomination of candidates and their election.

DISCUSSION

1   the primary issue

The primary issue, of course, is whether Seanad Éireann should continue to exist in any form, an issue which, as already noted, has been discussed inconclusively in the past. It is also considered in Appendix 7 – 'Notes On A New Irish Senate' by Professor Michael Laver. [Appendix 7 of the *Report of the Constitution Review Group* is included here as Annexe 2]. The need for a system of checks and balances on the legislative process and the need to bring as wide as possible a cross-section of society into the representative system suggest that the Seanad should be retained. An affirmative answer, also, is implied by the decision of the Government to give representation to emigrants in that House, a matter the Review Group has been expressly excused from attending to.

It must be acknowledged, however, that the Seanad in its current form has come in for criticism from different quarters, often accompanied by demands for its abolition. Particular criticism has been directed at the Seanad's arcane nomination and electoral procedure, and its almost total domination by the Dáil and the Government. In a modern state where efficient executive or legislative action, without undue complexity or confrontation, can be vital, this domination may be inescapable. As previous experience with investigatory committees and commissions indicates, these are difficult issues which the Review Group could not address in a satisfactory manner in the time available to it. A separate, comprehensive, independent review is necessary.

If the two main criteria for retention of the Seanad – the desirability of a system of checks and balances and of representation of as wide a cross-section of society as possible – cannot be satisfied by suitable reforms, then the case for a Seanad would fail and it should be abolished. In this event, it would be necessary to have its functions of representation and review performed by some other means, perhaps through reform of the legislative and representative role of the Dáil, for example by way of a suitably designed extension of Dáil membership, which could be considered in connection with reform of the Dáil electoral system.

2   functions

The system whereby a Seanad election automatically follows any Dáil election may make the two houses insufficiently distinct from one another. Consideration might therefore be given to decoupling Dáil and Seanad elections. It should be borne in mind, of course, that the conflict between the Senate and the Dáil in the 1930s led to the abolition of the Senate. Under the Constitution the Seanad is part of the institutional arrangement for legislating in the State and as such cannot be removed from party politics and cannot, in practice, differ too fundamentally in its basic political philosophy from the directly elected Dáil.

The system whereby the Taoiseach nominates a significant proportion of Senators identifies the Seanad very closely with the Government, while potentially undermining public perceptions of the representative role of the Seanad. Given a legislative process that in practice allows the Seanad little opportunity to obstruct the Government, nominations by the Taoiseach to strengthen the representation of Government parties in that house should not be a predominant concern. If the discretion is retained, it is desirable that more use should be made of it to allow entry to the Seanad of persons with special experience or qualifications, irrespective of political party allegiance.

Consideration might also be given to the possibility of finding new tasks for the Seanad that are not currently assigned within the political system.

3   composition

A fundamental justification for the existence of a second house is that it differs from the main house in its representative character. In a unitary state, this difference could be achieved by giving a voice to vocational, regional or other groupings of the various elements in society, including particularly those (for example women, the unemployed, lower socio-economic groups) not adequately represented at present in Dáil Éireann. As things stand, the candidature produced by the panel nomination procedure and by the nature of the electorate results not in a vocational Seanad, as originally envisaged, but in one not markedly different from Dáil Éireann. The panel system is clearly a reflection of the corporativist ideas which prevailed in the 1930s when the Constitution was enacted. The Seanad thus fails to satisfy the fundamental criterion specified above.

Alternative methods of providing a Seanad have been looked at by the Review Group – see the personal suggestions in papers by two members of the Review Group, Dr Kathleen Lynch (Appendix 6 – 'Seanad Éireann') and Professor Michael Laver (Appendix 7 – 'Notes on a new Irish Senate'). The Taoiseach's nominees have already been mentioned. [Appendices 6 and 7 of the *Report of the Constitution Review Group* are included here as Annexes 1 and 2].

Another obvious issue in relation to the current composition of the Seanad concerns university representation. The choice appears to lie between extending the franchise to graduates of all third-level institutions or abolishing such representation altogether. The undoubted quality of many of the university representatives and the value of the contribution they can make may no longer outweigh the case against reserving for any category of citizens a special political constituency. On the other hand, the proposed reservation of seats for emigrants, and reform of the Seanad generally, may involve a general move towards group representation.

4   functional and vocational representation

Functional and vocational representation in general presents issues that are both intriguing and complex. The current system of Seanad representation is in theory vocational but, as we have argued, in practice is not. A working system of functional and vocational representation could, however, provide a Seanad that did more than merely mirror the composition of the Dáil: it could make possible the representation of a wider cross-section of groups in society. It would, of course, be necessary to settle upon a set of groups to be represented that would meet with broad public support, and to devise a method of ensuring that such representation actually worked in practice, while preserving the necessary balance with the political system to ensure that government and legislature actually work. These are not easy issues to resolve, but are clearly ones that merit serious and careful thought.

5   MEPs and Northern Ireland representation

Other matters discussed in the appended working papers include: the representation or right of audience of members of the European Parliament; the position of Northern Ireland representatives.

Conclusion

The composition of the Seanad in itself is evidently too wide and complex an issue for effective examination within the time-limit set for completion of the Review Group's task. It should, therefore, be part of the recommended separate, comprehensive, independent review. To facilitate such a review the Review Group arranged for the updating of the tables at Annexes 21-23 of the Report of the Committee on the Constitution (1967) – see Appendix 8. [Appendix 8 of the *Report of the Constitution Review Group* is included here as Appendix III].

OTHER ISSUES

1   participation of Ministers in Seanad debates

There is some concern that it is usually Ministers of State rather than Cabinet Ministers who take part in Seanad debates. Given the Government, Dáil and European Union responsibilities of Ministers, a requirement that they must also attend the Seanad could be unrealistic.

2   parliamentary questions

While parliamentary questions can be a powerful lever for eliciting information from the Government, the Review Group considers, for reasons given in the preceding paragraph, that the privilege of asking such questions should continue to be reserved to members of Dáil Éireann, the house to which the Government is answerable under the Constitution.

3 citizenship

Article 18.2 requires that a member of Seanad Éireann must be a citizen. The Taoiseach's power to nominate has been used in recent times to provide Senators from Northern Ireland. Current provisions regarding citizenship would mean that increasingly fewer people from Northern Ireland would be eligible, as citizens, for such nomination. This might be considered in any review of the role of the Seanad.

4 resignation

When a Taoiseach resigns Ministers also resign. If the provision (Article 18.3) for nomination of Senators by the Taoiseach is retained, the question will arise as to whether, in those circumstances, the Senators nominated by the Taoiseach should also resign. This would also need to be considered in a general review.

5 postal ballot

Article 18.5 provides for secret postal ballot.

Recommendation

Delete the word 'postal' because it makes the process specifically dependent on the postal services.

6 general election

Article 18.8 does not envisage the possibility that a second general election might be called before the ninety days within which the Constitution provides that a Seanad election will take place, a possibility which would create a situation where a second Seanad election would have to be called before the first one was completed.

Recommendation

If the current sequence of Dáil and Seanad elections is retained, the Article should be amended to provide that the originally occasioned Seanad election should be aborted, and that an election related to the second Dáil dissolution should be held instead.

7 polling day

Article 18.9 does not define the polling day.

Recommendation

The latest date upon which an elector can vote should be regarded as the polling day.

8   a redundant Article?

Article 19 has not been used and consideration of it would fall within the recommended separate, comprehensive, independent review.

CONCLUSION

As constituted, the Seanad does not appear to satisfy the criteria for a relevant, effective and representative second house. There are fundamental political problems to be answered before a solution can be prescribed for the problem presented by the Seanad; moreover, there is a wide range of solutions that might be prescribed. Given the time, and the resources available, the Review Group cannot undertake a comprehensive and authoritative investigation of the Seanad's composition and role – such as that conducted by the previous commissions set up and organised specifically to consider these questions.

Recommendation

The Review Group recommends a separate, comprehensive, independent examination of all issues relating to Seanad Éireann. For this reason, no list of other recommendations, whether relating to substantive or technical issues, is provided, although some matters are suggested above for consideration in such a review. If such a review does not resolve the issue of representation and other substantive issues in a satisfactory manner, serious consideration will need to be given to the abolition of the Seanad and the transfer of its role and functions to other parts of the political system, as indicated above by the Review Group.

Annexe 1: The Seanad

Dr Kathleen Lynch

The problems concerning the Seanad as presently constituted will not be resolved substantively by way of the proposal for direct regional elections. The reason for this is because the system of election will result in the same type of political representation which is presently available through the Dáil (unless Northern Ireland is included as a constituency). Political parties, in other words, will present candidates for election in these large constituencies and the people who are likely to be nominated and to succeed are those with the kind of public profile that is required for success in the current European elections, mostly those who are well-known politicians already.

Given that the express remit of the Seanad is to a) provide a system of checks and balances on the legislative process and b) provide a voice for a cross section of opinion from all sectors of Irish life, it is not at all clear how a regionally constituted Senate would meet these two requirements. As the Senators would be drawn most likely from the same political parties which are represented in the Dáil, and would have been schooled in the values and practices of traditional party politics, it is unlikely that they would provide a critical and evaluative voice on legislation. Furthermore, and this is the most serious issue, the people who would be elected in this system would not provide a voice for those sectors of Irish society which are now poorly represented through the Dáil system, including women, working-class and unemployed people, people with a disability, and minority groups such as Travellers. In an open competitive situation such as direct regional elections, only candidates who are well known and have the time and resources to become well known will be elected: those without resources and without the means of establishing a high public profile would not be elected and this means that the principle enshrined in b) above would not be realised. It is for these reasons therefore that I would propose a different system of panels for the election of members to the Seanad.

The problem which is confronting Irish political life is that the system of representative democracy which is in operation fails to provide adequate representation for relatively large, and in some cases, vulnerable sectors of Irish society. The net effect of this has been that problems such as low pay, unemployment and emigration have not been seriously addressed by successive Governments.

In 1989 the ESRI report, *Poverty, Income and Welfare in Ireland,* based on the national Household Budget Survey of 1987, reported that almost one-third of the population was living on or below the poverty line (that is to say had an income which was 60% or less of the average industrial wage). The same research found that income differentials had grown between the late 1960s and the late 1980s. Women, children and households headed by the long-term unemployed are among the most vulnerable to poverty. Yet as noted in the research paper on Article 16, only 12% of TDs and Senators respectively are women, and those from low income or working class backgrounds are very poorly represented in both houses of the Oireachtas. If Irish society is serious about issues such as promoting gender equality, eliminating poverty as opposed to managing and containing it, ensuring equal status and respect for minorities as opposed to tolerating their existence, then it must ensure a system of political representation which would enable these large but poorly represented groups to have a voice. The Senate could be employed for this purpose, using an alternative panel system.

One of the reasons why the panel system as proposed in the 1937 Constitution has not been effective is because it is impossible to identify the electoral constituency for any given panel. This problem would be overcome if a different panel system was in operation. For example, a panel system could be developed based on the current concept of social partners which operates in a wide variety of fora including the National Economic and Social Forum, the Area Development Management System and the County Enterprise Boards. The panels would consist of all the registered members of the following organisations or groups:

panel 1	the employer and farming sectors (IBEC, IFA, ICMSA, SFA, Macra Na Feirme)
panel 2	National Women's Council of Ireland and all its affiliated organisations
panel 3	the Irish National Organisation of the Unemployed and other organisations representing welfare recipients
panel 4	the trade unions
panel 5	youth (18-25). The National Youth Council of Ireland and other youth groups such as Foroige
panel 6	older people over 65 (National Council for the Elderly)
panel 7	Northern Ireland
panel 8	TDs' and county councillors' nominees
panel 9	minority groups (Travellers, disabled people) ITM, DTEG, DFI
panel 10	MEPs
panel 11	emigrants

The panels would be reviewed every ten years by an independent commission.

Annexe 2: Notes on a new Irish Senate

Michael Laver

THE NEED FOR A NEW SENATE

Countries such as Ireland that operate a system of parliamentary government can be divided into those that have two houses and those that have only one. All federal states (Australia, Austria, Germany, Switzerland, for example) have two houses. In these, the lower house represents the interests of people as a whole, and makes and breaks Governments, while the upper house represents the interests of the constituent states. This particular rationale for an upper house is absent in a unitary state such as Ireland. Some unitary democracies have upper houses (Britain, France, Italy, Spain, for example) while others do not (Denmark, Finland, Iceland, Portugal, Norway, Sweden, for example). If Ireland had no upper house, therefore, it would be by no means unique.

In unitary states, the primary rationale for an upper house has to do with the system of checks and balances on the legislative process. If there is no upper house and particularly if, as in Ireland, the head of state has a largely formal non-political role, legislation that does not conflict with the Constitution requires only a majority in the lower house. A Government with a secure parliamentary majority can effectively legislate at will, constrained only by the Constitution. This offers scant protection for minorities (the protection of minorities is of course a fundamental feature of any democracy), and it offers no check on hasty and ill-considered action by the Government. For these reasons, many of those countries that do not have a senate have put in place some institutional framework that fulfils some of the functions of an upper house. Luxembourg has a Council of State, the members of which are appointed for life by the Grand Duke. The Norwegian parliament divides into two chambers after the election. In Finland and Portugal the lower house has a large and important committee that functions in some respects as a second chamber. Thus, if the Seanad were to be abolished, the matter of providing a system of checks and balances on the legislative process would have to be addressed.

However there are additional circumstances in Ireland that militate against abolition of the Seanad. These concern relations with Northern Ireland, and the range of possible constitutional settlements for the province to which many aspire. There is clearly a potential future role for the Seanad as a body that can provide a voice for a cross section of opinion from the whole island of Ireland. Abolishing the Seanad now would foreclose this potentially important element in a future constitutional settlement. Combining this argument with the need for some system of checks and balances on the legislative process, we have a strong case for the retention rather than the abolition of the Seanad. This implies, given the bulk of expert opinion that is critical of the current arrangements, that any serious review of the Irish Constitution should propose a new Seanad.

THE PROBLEM

The general problem can be simply stated. The current Seanad, despite having been graced by some worthy and able Senators over the years, has no clear role in the Irish political system and has a peculiar and indefensible system for selecting Senators. What needs to be done, therefore, is to provide a clear and worthwhile role for the Seanad, and to develop a system for choosing Senators that commands widespread popular respect.

More specifically, the Seanad's current shortcomings arise from the following problems, each of which should be addressed in any review of the Constitution:

i) *the Seanad is dominated by the Government.* This happens because the 'Taoiseach's eleven' nominees guarantee a Government majority (Article 18.1, 18.3). The current situation is the unique exception that proves the rule. For the first time in the history of the State, the current Government was formed without an intervening election. The current Taoiseach must thus live with the previous Taoiseach's nominees and the Government does not have a majority in the Seanad. As a direct result of this, the Seanad currently has a greater role in political life than before, shown in recent public debate over its possible rejection of legislation on abortion information and the potential for the State's first ever Article 27 referendum on the issue

ii) *the Seanad lives in the shadow of the Dáil.* This happens for two reasons. The first is that the Seanad is dissolved whenever the Dáil is dissolved and a Seanad election must follow every Dáil election (Article 18.8, 18.9). The second is a set of legislative procedures that gives the Dáil the final say in almost everything. The net result is to make the Seanad so subservient to the Dáil that its independent existence is currently hard to justify

iii) *rules for choosing Senators are bizarre and anachronistic* in both their general constitutional framework (Article 18.6, 18.7, Article 19) and their specific legislative enactment. With the obvious exception of the British House of Lords, they make the Irish Seanad the oddest upper house in Europe. The original corporatist aim of providing a forum for various vocational groups had been undermined by obscure provisions for nomination and election, combined with the tiny and elitist electorate for most seats. These give Irish Senators limited public legitimacy.

Any reform of the Seanad must therefore give it a role that is to some degree independent of both the Dáil and the Government of the day, and must provide a system of selecting Senators who can command widespread public respect.

ELEMENTS OF A SOLUTION

We need therefore to focus on the issues of how to choose members of the Seanad, and of what they should do once they have been chosen.

Selecting Senators

Senators can be chosen in one of three basic ways. They can be appointed. This is the case, for example, in the British House of Lords, with over 1000 members who are appointed for life by the Government of the day (or who inherited an appointment from their ancestors). It is also the case in the federal states of Germany, Austria and Switzerland, where the constituent state appoints members of the federal senate. Senators can be indirectly elected – in France and the Netherlands Senators are elected by members of local or provincial councils. Or they can be directly elected, as are the bulk of Senators in Belgium, Italy, and Spain.

The current system of choosing Irish Senators is an amalgam of two principles. The first is the British principle of using the Government appointment of members to ensure as far as possible a Government majority in the upper house and thereby remove its ability to undermine Government legislation. The second is a corporatist principle of representing vocational interests that has its roots very much in the Catholic social thinking and the corporate states of the 1930s, when the Irish Constitution was framed. Although no other western state now uses this representational principle, this is not a reason in itself to abandon it.

The difficulty is in realising the principle in practice. The current system clearly does not do so. The various vocational panels contribute merely to an arcane nomination process that is vocational in name only, while the current method of choosing most elected Senators is indirect election by an electorate of about 900 people comprising TDs, outgoing Senators and local councillors. The problem with reforming this system is that it would be difficult and intensely controversial, in an era of mass media and popular participation in public debate, to come up with an agreed set of vocational groups whose interests should be enshrined in the Constitution and guaranteed representation in the upper house. A further difficult problem is one of finding a set of vocational groups that divide the population so that everyone is a member of one group, but of only one group. In my view it would now be extremely contentious to attempt, in cold blood, to introduce an effective system of vocational representation in the Seanad. Nonetheless, it is a possibility that merits very serious consideration.

What are the alternatives? The Seanad could be a forum for the great and the good, a group of people of wisdom, achievement and experience, appointed in some manner by the political system. In my view, it would be almost impossible in a modern democratic era to justify introducing what would in effect be an Irish version of the House of Lords.

Senators could be appointed or elected by county councils, but the rationale for this in a unitary state such as Ireland is dubious, while county councils currently have no formal constitutional status. One possible indirect route to the Seanad that is intriguing and worth exploring is making Irish MEPs members of the Seanad. MEPs currently have no forum within Ireland, and are under no obligation to give an account of their actions other than at election time. This situation might be remedied by making them members of the Seanad.

Senators could be directly elected. The rationale for this option, in terms of democratic legitimacy, seems to me to be overwhelming. The problem that remains to be solved is that, if Seanad elections are tied to Dáil elections, and if the election to both houses is held on the same basis, then the two houses will be identical and there will be no point in having the second one. This strongly implies decoupling Dáil and Seanad elections, and/or holding Seanad elections on a different basis from Dáil elections.

Since the Seanad does not play, nor is it envisaged to play, a role in government formation in Ireland, there is absolutely no need for the Seanad to renew its mandate every time the Government falls. This suggests that Seanad elections should be held at fixed intervals, a provision that would immediately decouple Dáil from Seanad elections.

There are two ways to hold elections for the Seanad on a different basis from those for the Dáil. A different system of constituencies could be used. A different electoral system could be used.

In my view, it is not desirable to use different electoral systems for different elections in the same state, unless there are transparent reasons for doing so. People should feel that the electoral system they use is the most appropriate system, and this feeling will be undermined if two different systems are used simultaneously. Nonetheless, it is an option, and one possibility is to use Seanad elections to explore the impact in Ireland of an alternative electoral system to STV. This would allow an experiment with a new electoral system that did not involve experimenting with the very heart of the political process.

My preferred option, however, would be to retain the STV electoral system for the Seanad, with different constituencies. (As an aside it is worth noting that Senate rules for STV are actually more defensible than those for Dáil elections, since they involve looking at all votes cast when a surplus is transferred, rather than at certain bundles of votes only.) One possibility is to explore the possibility of a set of 'vocational' constituencies, as discussed above. If it is felt desirable to retain the more conventional notion of geographic constituencies, then these should be much larger than current Dáil constituencies, perhaps based on the traditional provinces, which do have social and cultural meaning for voters. These constituencies would each return twelve seats. (Note that 'fair' geographic representation of the population is provided by the Dáil, while Seanad representation can be used to guarantee a voice for particular sections of the population that might otherwise be unheard. The rationale for large constituencies is that they would allow for the election of minority voices that are presently unrepresented under the current system of 3-seat and 5-seat constituencies.)

A variant of this option, one that would no doubt be very controversial, would include Northern Ireland as one of the Seanad constituencies. This would serve the very desirable function of bringing Northern voices much closer to the mainstream of politics in the Republic, with obvious potential advantages. There will of course be legal and logistical problems with organising Seanad elections in Northern Ireland.

Summarising these conclusions:

i) the provision for the Taoiseach to nominate Senators should be abolished

ii) Seanad elections should be held at fixed intervals

iii) the current provisions for nominating candidates for Seanad elections and for electing Senators should be replaced entirely

iv) qualifications and procedures for nomination to the Seanad should be the same as for nomination to the Dáil

v) The system of constituencies should be replaced entirely. Either these should represent an agreed set of vocational interests, or four large geographic areas, as follows:

   a) Munster

   b) Leinster (minus Dublin)

   c) Dublin

   d) Connacht/Ulster (Connacht, Donegal, Cavan, Monaghan)

vi) consideration should be given to creating an additional Seanad constituency for Northern Ireland, or to making Northern Ireland's Westminster MPs members of the Seanad

vii) consideration should also be given to making Irish MEPs members of the Seanad.

What should the Seanad do?

In a unitary state, as we have seen, the main role for a senate is as part of the system of checks and balances on the legislative process. At present, the Seanad hardly figures at all in this. The two powers that the Seanad has are the ability to delay non-Money Bills for ninety days, and provision under Article 27 for a joint petition to the President for a referendum on a Bill by a majority of the Seanad and one-third of the Dáil. Neither of these has any practical effect in a situation in which the Government almost invariably has a majority in the Seanad. The powers of delay have rarely been used; Article 27 has never been used.

The abolition of the Taoiseach's eleven nominees and the decoupling of Dáil and Seanad elections, as recommended above, would in themselves go some way towards breathing life into existing powers. As noted above, the fact that the current Government was not formed after an election in effect creates the situation in which the Seanad would typically find itself after these reforms. The Government cannot guarantee Seanad rubber-stamping of its legislation willy-nilly, while the real possibility exists of invoking Article 27 if an issue arises uniting a majority of the Seanad and one-third of the Dáil. Reforming the basis of Seanad representation would thus in itself enhance the role of the Seanad in the legislative system.

Further reforms of the Seanad's role and functioning are, however, much needed. Many commentators and committees have pointed to serious ambiguities in the system for passing Bills between the Dáil and Seanad, leading to the current possibility that Bills can fall inadvertently into a legislative limbo. This system should clearly be cleaned up, and in the process the role of the Seanad could be enhanced by rules with the effect that the period of time of the Seanad to delay implementation of legislation that it does not approve (with the exception of the annual budget) should be increased to 180 days. This is entirely defensible in terms of the need for the mature consideration of legislation, and would mean that the Seanad's powers of delay would have to be taken more seriously by the Dáil.

While it probably makes no practical difference, the position of Senators vis-à-vis TDs is demeaned by the provision (Article 28.7.2°) that no more than two Senators may be members of the Government. Constraints on government membership in Ireland follow the British model and are probably more severe than in most other European countries, where government membership is typically not confined to legislators. (In France, for example, a member of the government may not be a legislator and a legislator who is appointed to the government must give up his or her seat.) There is no good reason not to allow Irish Governments to comprise members of the Dáil and Seanad without restriction, save that the government formation process heavily implies that the Taoiseach is a member of the Dáil.

A further way to enhance the role of the Seanad would be to increase the obligation of the Government to give an account of itself in the upper house. This could be done by imposing stricter obligations on Government Ministers to make statements in the Seanad and to answer both verbal and written questions from Senators, though such a reform is more a matter for legislation and standing orders than for the Constitution.

The reforms discussed above in effect concern the recasting of existing powers, but the question also arises of whether the Seanad should be given new powers. It is undesirable for the Seanad to have powers that might place it in a situation of irreconcilable conflict with either the Dáil or the Government, since this would result in an inability to make decisions on potentially vital matters. However, the Seanad could be given the power to do things that need to be done, but which are not being done at present by any branch of the formal political system.

One example of a possible new power along these lines is the review of senior public appointments. Since 1937 there has been a relentless shift of the locus of key parts of public administration away from the core civil service towards the semi-state sector and other public bodies. Appointments to such bodies are increasingly important yet, while the core civil service is publicly accountable to the Dáil through the Minister in charge of the department concerned, there is very little public accountability for those holding other senior public positions. Giving the Seanad a role in reviewing appointments to such positions could introduce an element of public scrutiny over them. Obviously, other new powers could be considered, but the review of senior public appointments strikes me as something that would be popular, is much needed and would give the Seanad an important new job that was quite distinct from the current responsibilities of the Dáil.

To summarise, the Seanad's role could be enhanced as follows:

i) Article 27 should be retained

ii) there should be fundamental reform and simplification of the role of the Seanad in the legislative process, the net effect of which reform should be that the Seanad has the power to delay non-Money Bills by 180 days

iii) the provision that only two Senators may be members of the Government should be removed (Article 28.7.2°). No upper limit should be placed on this

iv) the obligations of members of the Government to give an account of their actions to the Seanad, and to answer parliamentary questions posed by Senators, should be clarified and extended

v) consideration should also be given to endowing the Seanad, or Seanad committees, with some additional functions. One obvious possibility is to give it a role in the review of senior public appointments outside the core bureaucracy.

CONCLUSIONS

The new Irish Seanad would be independent of the Government and the Dáil. It would give a voice to both broad strands of opinion and minority viewpoints that currently don't get a formal hearing in the Irish political system. And it should have a clear and rational legitimacy. While the Dáil would be the sole body responsible for making and breaking Governments, and would retain the final say on legislation, the Seanad's sanction of a 180 day delay in the enactment of legislation, combined with the possibility of Article 27 referendums, would mean that the voice of the Seanad could not be ignored. Reform of the Irish Seanad along the lines suggested above should thus result in a body that was a far more vibrant and useful part of Irish political life.

Appendix II

Options for the future of Seanad Éireann

John Coakley (UCD) and Michael Laver (TCD)

1 INTRODUCTION

This paper sets out to provide a structure within which possible future roles for Seanad Éireann can be reviewed in a balanced and systematic way. The need for such a review is quite widely felt both within and without the political establishment, and this feeling was recently brought to a head in the conclusions about the Seanad reached by the Constitution Review Group: 'the Review Group recommends a separate, comprehensive, independent examination of all issues relating to Seanad Éireann'. The reason for this conclusion was that '[a]s constituted, the Seanad does not appear to satisfy the criteria for a relevant, effective and representative second house'. The stark implication that was drawn was that '[i]f such a review does not resolve the issue of representation and other substantive issues in a satisfactory manner, serious consideration will need to be given to the abolition of the Seanad and the transfer of its role and functions to other parts of the political system ...' (Constitution Review Group, 1996a: 71).

Obviously a single paper such as this can never aspire to provide a comprehensive independent examination of all issues relating to the Seanad.[1] Indeed it would not be appropriate for us to do this, since such a review is properly the job of those with the political mandate to conduct it. Our aim in this paper, therefore, is to carry out some of the basic groundwork that might facilitate such a review.

Our first task is to set Seanad Éireann in the context of the role and functioning of upper houses in other parliamentary democracies, looking not only at unitary states such as Ireland, but also at federal states such as Germany or Australia. Although the role of the second chamber may be radically different in federal states, we may still have much to learn from them. As we shall see, the Seanad is in some respects a rather unusual upper house, and the experience of other countries will be vital in any attempt to review its future. Section 2 of this paper thus looks at the role and functions of second chambers in the contemporary world, utilising the Inter-Parliamentary Union's very extensive on-line database, which deals in some detail with upper houses, to provide an up-to-date summary of the position in November 1996. To the best of our knowledge, this invaluable source of information has not previously been systematically explored in this way in any other country.

Set against this international context, the evolution of Seanad Éireann to the present day is summarised in section 3, which also reviews the Seanad's current role and functions. At the end of this section, we summarise what we take to be the current core critique that has led to calls for a review of the position. This critique is not that the Seanad is failing in the role that it has

---

[1] Quite apart from anything else, this paper was commissioned and written over a short period of time, and many aspects of it would have been extended had additional time and resources been available

been given, but rather that its current role and functions are of insufficient importance to justify retaining an entire second house of the legislature. This critique is what leads to calls for the Seanad's abolition or reform.

We explore the implications for the Irish political system of abolishing or reforming Seanad Éireann in section 4, in which the main substantive arguments of this paper are developed. In this section, as in each of the sections that follow, we structure our discussion in terms of two important features of second chambers: their composition, by which we mean the principles according to which they are selected, and the powers that they have at their disposal.[2] In section 4, therefore, we review future options for both the composition and the powers of the Seanad. We finish this section with an exploration of the possible political consequences of various ways in which the composition and powers of a future Seanad might interact with each other in a working second chamber.

In section 5, we draw together the discussion in the previous sections in a set of conclusions that outlines what we take to be some feasible options which merit further exploration in any comprehensive review of the future of Seanad Éireann. The final evaluation of these options, of course, is a job for the political system. In the last section, section 6, we reinforce some of the points that have emerged in the earlier parts of this study.

2 THE ROLE OF SECOND CHAMBERS IN THE MODERN STATE

In evaluating the political role and future of Seanad Éireann, we must begin by reviewing the general role of second chambers in modern parliaments, to

---

[2] In this we follow the thrust of the Constitution Review Group's report, which identified these two primary issues but which withheld detailed comment on either:

> The rationale for having two houses of parliament in a unitary state is based upon two important features of any mature democracy. The first is the need to take account of political interests that may not be adequately represented in the main house; the second is the need for some final review of legislative proposals before they become binding on all. The so-called lower house is the primary legislature, representing the people generally and making or breaking governments. The primary purpose of an upper house is to provide a system of checks and balances on the legislative process. This can be done with more assurance if the composition of the upper house does not simply mirror that of the lower house (Constitution Review Group, 1996:66-67)

see what lessons we can learn from the experience of other countries.[3]

Before doing this, however, we must first make a point about terminology. We have used the term 'second chamber' or 'upper house' to refer to that house of parliament which typically does not have the primary representative function of the 'lower' house and typically has the lesser role in the legislative and governmental process. While these bodies are generally called 'senates', a range of alternative descriptions is available.[4] Furthermore, it is by no means always clear whether a particular body is, in fact, a second chamber or whether it falls outside the remit of parliament.[5]

2.1 Introductory overview

When the Committee on the Constitution reported its views on Seanad Éireann in 1967, it felt able to conclude that in having a second chamber Ireland resembled 'most modern democracies' (Committee on the Constitution, 1967: 26). Subsequent comparative studies have, however, shown a steady decline in the proportion of parliaments with second

---

[3] As the editor of a recent standard collection of essays on parliaments observed:

> ... in recent years there appears to have been something of a tendency for legislatures to establish committees to consider major structural – indeed, constitutional – reform and for those committees to look beyond their own shores for inspiration. Indeed, in some respects, legislative committees vested with the task of legislative reform appear to have been ahead of the academic community in comparative analysis (Norton, 1990: 14)

For general overviews, see texts cited elsewhere here; for earlier surveys, Ameller, 1966 and Paxton 1975. For vigorous and balanced discussions of second chambers, see Mill, 1912: 335-343, and Wheare, 1966: 132-146

[4] Of 58 second chambers in November 1996, 43 are called 'senates' (or its equivalent in the local official language). Other designations are Federal Council (Austria, Ethiopia, Germany), Council of the Federation (Russia), Council of States (India, Switzerland), House of Peoples (Bosnia and Herzegovina), National Council (Namibia, Nepal), House of Councillors (Japan), House of Representatives (Burkina Faso), Assembly of People's Representatives (Kyrghyzstan), First Chamber (Netherlands), House of Lords (United Kingdom) and House of Counties (Croatia)

[5] In the present report, we have followed convention in including such bodies as the German Federal Council (*Bundesrat*), while excluding the Luxembourg Council of State (*Conseil d'État*) and the Slovene National Council (*drzavni zbor*). According to the German constitution, parliament consists of a single chamber, the Federal Diet (*Bundestag*); the Federal Council (*Bundesrat*) is a forum to represent the states (*Länder*), but this is normally classified as a second chamber of parliament. The position within the European Union is similar, but there the Council of Ministers is not conventionally seen as a second chamber. We have also treated as unicameral such bodies as the Norwegian *Storting*, which on its election divides into two subchambers, the *Lagting* and the *Odelsting*. The difficulty of placing parliaments in one category or the other is illustrated by the Slovene National Council, which plays a significant watchdog role in the legislative and other domains; for a defence of the view that it constitutes a second chamber, see Kristan, 1996

chambers.[6] By October 1996, the Inter-Parliamentary Union's database recorded that this proportion had dropped just below one third (58 out of 178), though in November 1996 an additional second chamber appeared, in the Czech Republic. While part of this decline arises from the creation of new countries with unicameral parliaments, the decline of second chambers is also reflected in the abolition of these bodies in such cases as New Zealand (1950), Denmark (1953) and Sweden (1969).

The origins of multicameral legislatures lie in the notion of estate representation as it evolved in the middle ages. This rested on an assumption that the different legally defined 'orders', 'estates' or classes within society were entitled to presence or at least representation in the legislative body, whether grouped in two houses as in Great Britain, in three as in France or in four as in Sweden (see Marongiu, 1968; Myers, 1975). The modern democratic revolution swept this system away, replacing it by the radically different principle of individual rather than corporate representation. Finland represents the first and purest example of this transition: in 1906 its four-chambered diet (representing respectively nobility, clergy, burghers and peasants) was replaced by a modern parliament, elected by direct, equal, secret and universal suffrage.[7]

While the trend towards democratically elected unicameral bodies was clearly very powerful, a second house of parliament did survive in many cases alongside the popularly elected lower house. There was an obvious reason for this in federal states. Federations, especially loose ones, are unions not just of people but also of territories; and there is a long-established case for the separate representation of territories in the legislature. But other factors have also played a part in securing the survival of second chambers. There are *representational* arguments based on the need to ensure that special interests are represented in parliament. There are *institutional* arguments based on the need to provide a body for additional deliberation on legislation. Finally, there are essentially *political* arguments based either on conservatism, for example the need to counteract the effects of public opinion as represented in the lower house, or on institutional inertia and the view that, because the second chamber has existed for a long time, it should continue to exist.

In general, the case for a second chamber in federal states is overwhelming. As may be seen from Table 1, 82% of federal states (18 out of 22) have a

---

[6] Surveys by the Inter-Parliamentary Union over the following decades showed the proportion dropping to 46% (26 out of 56; Herman, 1976), 34% (28 out of 83; Inter-Parliamentary Union, 1986) and 33% (58 out of 178; Inter-Parliamentary Union, 1996); see also Wheare, 1968; Blondel, 1973; Laundy, 1989)

[7] This constitutional revolution, to which the contemporary Finnish parliament traces its origins, was all the more remarkable because of the acquiescence of the head of state, the Grand Duke of Finland – who was also the autocratic Tsar Nicholas II of Russia, with which Finland had been linked since 1809 in a personal union

second chamber, as opposed to 26% of unitary states (40 out of 156).[8] Furthermore, the only federal states that do not have a second chamber are small in size and population, three of them having fewer than one million inhabitants.[9] In larger and more diverse federal states, the case for a chamber representing the component units of the federation is widely seen as unanswerable.

Table 1: Second chambers in unitary and federal states, 1996

Type of state	Unicameral legislature	Bicameral legislature	Total
Unitary	116	40	156
Federal	4	18	22
Total	120	58	178

Note: these data refer to countries on which information is maintained by the Inter-Parliamentary Union

Source: computed from sources cited in annexe 1

None of this means that there is any necessary connection between population size and the existence of a second chamber. It is true that the average population of countries with bicameral parliaments (47 million) is much greater than that of countries with unicameral ones (24 million). The group of unicameral states, however, includes such giants as China (population 1.2 billion), while the group of federal states includes nine countries with a population of less than one million.[10] There are 17 states which have a smaller population than Ireland but which nonetheless have a second chamber.

2.2 Composition

Unlike lower (or 'first') houses of parliament, upper (or 'second') chambers tend to vary enormously in their composition. We summarise the principal characteristics of these bodies in annexe 1, and comment on their principal features below. Debate about the composition of Seanad Éireann has covered a number of matters, though the most important concerns the principles according to which it is selected. Two related issues are the link between the

---

8   The distinction between unitary and federal states is not always clear cut; we have followed here the conventional distinction, accepting constitutional descriptions that are either explicit and primary (incorporated in the text of the constitution) or implicit and secondary (derived from other sources)

9   The states in question are Comoros (population 470,000), Saint Kitts and Nevis (41,000), the Federated States of Micronesia (121,000) and United Arab Emirates (1,861,000). These population figures, and those used elsewhere in this text, refer to 1994 population data as available in United Nations, 1996

10   The smallest are Palau (17,000), Antigua and Barbuda (65,000) and Grenada (92,000)

timing of Seanad and Dáil elections, and the size of the Seanad itself. In reviewing the 58 extant second chambers, therefore, we focus on three of their characteristics:

- their principle of selection
- their cycle of renewal, and the relationship of this to the renewal of the popularly elected chamber, and
- their size, relative to the popularly elected house and to the population.

2.2.1 The selection of members of the second chamber

In the modern democratic state, it is assumed that the lower house of parliament will be elected in a rather specific way: by *direct*, *equal* and *secret* voting on the basis of *universal* suffrage. A few second chambers are elected on a similar basis, but in general second chambers are much more heterogeneous in their composition, and depart from one, two, three or all four of the principles mentioned above. Indeed, we frequently find second chambers which use a mixture of methods of selection.

We can classify the principles for selecting members of second chambers into at least eight categories. First, they may be selected by *direct election*, either in the same manner as the lower house or in accordance with an alternative set of rules. Second, they may be selected by *indirect election* by a tier of voters at a lower level, such as local councillors, who represent the population, either as a whole or as divided into territorial units. Third, in a variant of this, members of a senate may be indirectly elected to represent functional or vocational groups, in a form of *corporate representation*. Fourth, they may be selected by members of the other chamber – *selection by the lower house*. Fifth, they may be selected, in part at least, by their own colleagues in the upper house – *cooptation*. Sixth, they may be appointed by a single individual, normally the head of state – the pure principle of *appointment*. Seventh, this appointment may extend not merely for a fixed term or even for a lifetime, but may be extended to descendants – the principle of *heredity*, which can, of course, also originate other than by appointment. Finally, a special variant of the principle of appointment is that of ex officio membership, where past or present appointment to a particular office carries the additional privilege of membership of the second chamber.

We now review the operation of these methods for selecting second chambers, in order of their relative importance, noting that more than one method is used in many second chambers.[11] When only one method is used for the selection of a second chamber this is most often direct election (16

---

[11] We should also point out that in our universe of 58 second chambers we include not only bodies that have functioned effectively over many decades, such as the British House of Lords and the US senate, but also bodies whose existence as functioning entities may be open to question, either because their structure is currently being overhauled or because of local political circumstances. Even in such cases, though, constitutional provisions may give guidance regarding the options for second chambers

cases), followed by indirect election (13) and appointment (13). In the remaining 16 cases a combination of principles is used, though one may be clearly dominant.[12]

DIRECT ELECTION In a considerable number of cases, and especially in unitary states, direct elections to the second chamber follow the pattern of representation in the lower house, including the conditions that *suffrage is universal* and *votes are equal*. In some cases, an identical electoral procedure is used, as in the Assembly of People's Representative of Kyrghyzstan (majority system), the senate of Palau (plurality system) and the senate of Romania (party list system).[13]

We also find states in which all aspects of elections to the two chambers are identical except for the electoral formula itself. Examples are the Dominican Republic, whose senate is elected by means of the plurality system in single-member constituencies whereas the Chamber of Deputies is elected according to the party list system of proportional representation; and Colombia and Paraguay, whose senates are elected at national level by means of the party list system, whereas their House of Representatives and Chamber of Deputies respectively are elected from 33 and 18 multi-member constituencies according to the same system.[14] Japan is another example: 152 members of the House of Councillors are elected from multi-member constituencies (limited vote system) while 100 are elected from a single nationwide constituency (party list system); in the case of the House of Representatives, 300 are elected from single-member districts (plurality system) while 200 are elected from multi-member constituencies (party list system).[15]

In yet another variant, we find the special case of the Philippines, whose senate is elected by means of the plurality system from a single nationwide constituency, but whose House of Representatives includes, in addition to 204 directly elected members (party list), 46 appointees of the President of

---

12 In the discussion below we also refer briefly to electoral systems used in the selection of second chambers. In this context we use conventional terminology. Proportional representation by means of the single transferable vote and the party list system are well known. The plurality system refers to that in which the winning candidate is the one who gets most votes; the majority system is one in which the winning candidate gets a majority of votes cast (i.e. 50% or more), and is normally a two-ballot system, with a second election scheduled for a date shortly after the first; and under the limited vote system constituencies are multi-member but each voter has *fewer* votes than there are vacancies

13 In Romania, however, the qualifying age for senators is higher than that for deputies (35 as opposed to 23)

14 In the Colombian senate there are two additional senators to represent the indigenous communities

15 The House of Councillors is further differentiated from the House of Representatives in that its members are elected for a six-year term, one half retiring every three years

the Republic.[16]   While, strangely, the second chamber appears to be the more democratic in this case, the minimum qualifying age for senators is higher than for deputies (35 years as opposed to 25).

The second major type of direct election is one in which, while votes are equal, *suffrage is not universal*. The normal restriction is the minimum age required to qualify as an elector. In the Italian senate, which also has a small appointed and ex officio component, voters are required to be at least 25 years old, although only 18 for the Chamber of Deputies. Under the Irish Free State constitution of 1922, the minimum age for inclusion in the Senate electorate was 30, rather than 21 as for the Dáil.

In the third category of direct election, suffrage is universal but *votes are not equal:* seats are allocated according to territory rather than following the distribution of the population. This system is very typically found in federal states; all territorial components in the federation, with the possible exception of the federal capital territory, have equal representation in the second chamber, regardless of their population. The senates of the United States, Mexico, Brazil and Argentina, all elected according to the plurality system, are examples; so too is the Australian senate, elected by means of the single transferable vote system of proportional representation. But the equal representation of territories in the second chamber is not confined to federal states; in the Bolivian, Haitian and Polish senates (operating respectively modified plurality, majority and pure plurality systems) territories are represented equally.

INDIRECT ELECTION There are many countries in which the senate is said in common parlance to be indirectly elected: the people do not select its members directly, but their representatives do so on their behalf. Strictly speaking, no second chamber fully conforms to this format; there is none for which an electoral college or colleges mandated to select senators is specifically elected for this purpose, on the model of the electoral college that selects the President of the United States. Instead, so-called indirect election may be based upon selection by regional governments (as in the German Federal Council), by provincial assemblies (as in the First Chamber in the Netherlands) or by departmental electoral colleges including representatives of local councillors (as in France).[17]

In many cases, indirectly elected second chambers are based on the equal representation of territorial units. This is especially the case in federal states

---

[16] The appointed members of the Philippines House of Representatives include representatives of indigenous but non-religious minority groups (such as the urban poor, the peasantry, women and youth); these representatives are to be elected after 1998

[17] The size of the electorate varies enormously; opposite extremes are represented by Germany, where the electoral body (if it can be so described) is very small (the governments of the 16 *Länder*) and France, where the electoral college consists of 145,000 persons, made up overwhelmingly of municipal councillors but including also councillors at higher levels and deputies of the National Assembly (see France: Senate, 1996)

– Ethiopia, Pakistan and Russia for instance – though special provision may be made for federal or federally-administered territories. However, we find the same principle at work in unitary states, such as the Congo, Namibia and South Africa.

In other cases, indirect election is weighted according to population, as in Austria and Yugoslavia among federal states, or France, Mauritania and the Netherlands among unitary ones.[18] It is not always easy to make a clear-cut distinction between the territorial and the population principle in matters of representation; we also find cases where the unit of representation is territorial but the distribution of representatives takes partial account of population. Examples are the German Federal Council, where each *Land* is represented by between three and six voting members, depending on but not proportional to population, and the House of Peoples of Bosnia and Herzegovina, where the Serb Republic has five representatives and the Bosnian-Croat Federation has ten (five Bosnians and five Croats).[19]

Finally, in a few cases indirect election is a secondary principle in a chamber composed principally on the basis of some other mechanism. In the National Council of Nepal, for instance, 15 (out of 60) members are elected by the development regions (using the single transferable vote system of proportional representation), while in Belgium and Spain significant numbers are elected indirectly: 21 (out of 74) by the community councils in Belgium and 48 (out of 256) by the assemblies of the autonomous communities in Spain.

APPOINTMENT In many cases, especially in countries that have been under British political influence, the second chamber is appointed by the head of state. This principle can apply even in federal states. The Canadian senate is an example; its members are appointed until the age of seventy-five (or, up to 1965, for life) by the governor general on the advice of the prime minister, though, interestingly, the notion of regional representation is retained.[20] In

---

[18] In France and in Mauritania, rather unusually, provision is made for the representation of citizens resident abroad—12 in the case of France, and 3 in Mauritania. In France, these senators are elected by the Upper Council for French Persons Abroad. This is a public body presided over by the Minister of Foreign Affairs and composed of: (1) 150 members elected by French persons settled outside France; (2) persons (20 at most) appointed by the Minister by reason of their competencies in matters concerning the general interests of France abroad; (3) a representative of French persons settled in the principality of Andorra; and (4) 12 senators representing French persons settled outside France (France: Senate, 1996)

[19] This classification in the case of indirect election is crude, in that there is a case for placing others of the countries identified here as following either the territorial or the population principle in the intermediate category

[20] However, most of the regions do not coincide with the federal provinces. Four regions are represented by twenty-four senators each: Ontario, Quebec, Maritime Provinces and Western Provinces; the first two of these are provinces, but the two others are groupings of provinces. Newfoundland is represented by six, while the Northwest Territories and Yukon have one each (Canada: Parliament, 1996)

eight small West Indian or Caribbean states, the senates are similarly appointed, but in these cases the governor general (or, in one case, the President) acts on the advice of the prime minister for most appointments, and on that of the leader of the opposition for others. In these cases, provision is sometimes made for appointments based on advice from other bodies, or at the head of state's own discretion.[21]

In other cases, there are fewer restrictions on the capacity of the head of state to appoint members of the second chamber. Examples are the senates of Burkina Faso (appointed by the president) and of Thailand (appointed by the king, subject only to the requirement that none be party members). In Fiji, the president appoints twenty-four senators on the nomination of the Council of Chiefs, nine on the advice of the Rotuma Island Council and one at his own discretion, with particular regard to minority communities.[22] In Jordan the king appoints the senate, but he is obliged to select its members from clearly defined elite categories, such as former or current senior political and military office holders.

Aside from the bodies mentioned above, which are entirely appointed, the appointive principle is the dominant but not exclusive one in other bodies. The two clear examples are Malaysia, where the Supreme Head of the Federation appoints most of the senators (43; 26 are indirectly elected) and Swaziland, where the king again appoints a majority (20; 10 are selected by the House of Assembly). Although the British House of Lords is technically dominated by hereditary members, most of its active members are in fact nominated: they have been created life peers by the queen on the advice of the prime minister.

In yet other cases, the head of state makes a small number of appointments to chambers that are selected predominantly on some other basis. The president does so in Chile (6 senators), Croatia (5), India (12), Italy (9) and Kazakhstan (7), while the king does so in Lesotho (11) and Nepal (10). We

[21] This procedure is followed in the following countries, where the numbers appointed on the advice of the prime minister and of the leader of the opposition, respectively, are indicated in brackets: Antigua and Barbuda (11, 4); Bahamas (9, 4); Barbados (12, 2); Belize (5, 2); Grenada (7, 3); Jamaica (13, 8); Saint Lucia (6,3) and Trinidad and Tobago (16, 6). In some cases, the Governor General makes additional appointments: in Antigua and Barbuda, at his own discretion (1) and on the advice of the Barbuda Council (1); in the Bahamas on the advice of the prime minister after consulting with the leader of the opposition (3); in Barbados at his own discretion to represent such interests as he considers appropriate (7); in Belize after consultation with the Belize Advisory Council (3); in Grenada on the advice of the prime minister after consulting with interests he considers should be represented (3); in Saint Lucia after consultation with religious, economic and social groups (2); and in Trinidad and Tobago the President appoints additional senators at his own discretion from outstanding persons from economic, social or community organisations (9)

[22] This formulation is particularly important, in that it gives the indigenous Fijian population (49 per cent of the total) a controlling influence in the upper house. In the House of Representatives, ethnic Fijians are allocated 37 of the 70 seats

may add to this the peculiar case of Ireland where, uniquely, the appointive function rests with the head of government rather than with the head of state: the Taoiseach appoints 11 senators.[23]

HEREDITY The oldest of all principles of representation in multicameral legislatures was that of heredity, but this has tended to disappear as the whole notion of estate-based representation vanished in the twentieth century. Yet there remain two states where this is, at least technically, the dominant principle in the composition of the second chamber: one new second chamber in a traditional society (the senate of Lesotho) and one ancient chamber in a modern, industrialised society (the House of Lords of the United Kingdom). In both of these cases, though, this principle is qualified by that of appointment, and in the United Kingdom a majority of hereditary peers do not attend parliament, thus greatly reducing the de facto significance of the hereditary component.

CORPORATE REPRESENTATION Corporate representation is also close in its origins to traditional estate representation, but it represents a modernised form of this. This developed most fully in Catholic societies in the interwar period. It was not confined to these, however; the Estonian constitution of 1936 made provision for the election of a corporate second chamber, the Council of State.[24] There were two outstanding examples in interwar Europe. The Chamber of Fasci and Corporations in Italy, which replaced the Chamber of Deputies in 1939, consisted of the 150 members of the National Council of the Fascist Party and 500 effective members of the National Council of Corporations. This was, in fact, the *first* chamber of parliament; the old senate, whose members consisted of princes of the royal family and senators nominated for life by the king, continued to exist alongside the new chamber. The Corporative Chamber in Portugal was similar in composition but dissimilar in powers: it consisted of over 80 members from 25 designated functional or vocational areas (including agriculture, industry, commerce, religion, education, political life, administration and the arts), but its powers were merely consultative. It could report on Bills but did not participate directly in the legislative process.

The only surviving example of this form of representation at national level is the Irish Senate, 43 of whose members are indirectly elected to represent five vocational groups or panels. An additional six senators are elected by

---

23 This procedure was anticipated in 1922, when as a transitional measure the President of the Executive Council (prime minister) appointed half of the members of the first Senate

24 This consisted of 6 ex-officio representatives (the chief of staff of the army, the heads of the two largest churches, the rectors of two higher education institutions, and a representative of banking); 24 elected representatives (three from rural municipalities; one from urban municipalities; 16 from functional groups, including agriculture and fisheries, industry and trades, employees, urban property owners, free professions and the domestic sector; and one each from the defence militia, the educational sector, the national minorities and the health service); and 10 nominees of the President of the Republic (Uluots and Klesment, 1937)

university graduates, thus contributing to the strength of 'cultural and educational' interests (because of this, the Cultural and Educational panel is represented by only five indirectly elected senators; other panels range from seven to eleven members). A second surviving example, though not at national level, is the senate of the Free State of Bavaria, which is elected by vocational groups corresponding to 10 functional areas for a six-year term, one-third retiring every three years. This is a non-party body; areas represented are agriculture and forestry (11 senators), industry and commerce (5), trades (5), trade unions (11), liberal professions (4), cooperatives (5), religious communities (5), charitable organisations (5), universities (3) and local authorities (6). Another example at national level, but one which is not quite a second chamber, is the National Council of Slovenia. Modelled on the Bavarian senate, this 40-member body consists of 18 representatives of functional groups (social, economic, trade and professional interests), together with 22 representatives of local interests.[25]

SELECTION BY MEMBERS OF THE LOWER HOUSE In one case, Nepal, most members of the second chamber, the National Council, are elected by the first chamber, the House of Representatives (these 35 members are elected by the single transferable vote system of proportional representation). In Pakistan, 8 senators are elected by a portion of the National Assembly: the members who represent the federally administered tribal areas. In other cases, all members of the first chamber may be involved in the election as part of electoral colleges, but they are overwhelmed numerically by local councillors (France and Ireland are examples). In the Senate of the Irish Free State, from 1928 onwards senators were elected by Dáil deputies and existing senators, and half of the members of the first senate in 1922 were elected by the Dáil.

EX OFFICIO MEMBERSHIP In a number of cases, holders of certain posts enjoy senate membership ex officio. The law lords (senior judges who have been ennobled) in the British House of Lords are an example, as are the bishops and archbishops of the Church of England, who also sit ex officio in this chamber. In other countries, former presidents are ex officio members: Chile, Italy, Kazakhstan, Uruguay and Venezuela are examples.

COOPTATION Of necessity, this cannot be the dominant principle in representation (unless a minority is allowed to coopt a majority), but it can play an important role in certain cases. Belgium is an example – the newly elected senators coopt an additional 10 members.

---

[25] The composition of the National Council is as follows: 4 representatives of employers; 4 representatives of employees; 4 representatives of farmers, small business persons and independent professionals, 2 of whom represent farmers; 6 representatives of non-profit making organisations of which one represents the universities and high schools, one represents the area of education, one the area of research activities, one the area of sport and culture, one the medical field and one represents social care; and 22 representatives of local interests, elected by local councillors, employers, employees, farmers, small businesses, professionals and non-profit organisations, together with 22 representatives of local interests elected by local councillors (Slovenia: National Council, 1996)

Table 2 summarises the wide variety of approaches to selecting second chambers, together with the dominant principle of representation in each. The importance of direct elections, whether to represent people or territories, emerges clearly from this table: 24 second chambers are selected predominantly by this means, while 15 are indirectly elected. It should be noted that, while there is some relationship between the dominant principle of selection and the unitary or federal organisation of the state, the relationship is not a strong one.

Table 2: Dominant principle of representation in second chambers, 1996

Principle	Unitary states	Federal states	Total
1 Direct election: population	10	0	10
2 Direct election: territory	6	8	14
3 Indirect election: population	3	4	7
4 Indirect election: territory	4	4	8
5 Appointment	13	2	15
6 Heredity	2	0	2
7 Election by lower house	1	0	1
8 Vocationalism	1	0	1
Total	40	18	58

Note: category 2 includes Spain and Belgium, where large proportions are indirectly elected, and category 5 includes Malaysia, where a large proportion is indirectly elected. The qualifiers 'population' and 'territory' refer respectively to the distribution of seats in the second chamber – whether these follow the distribution of the population, or are allocated to territories on a basis of equality, regardless of population

Source: computed from sources cited in annexe 1

Finally, we noted in passing another feature that frequently distinguishes the composition of first and second chambers: the age threshold for eligibility. In the cases considered above, the minimum age requirement for membership of the lower house is normally higher than the minimum age requirement for voting. It usually ranges between 18 and 21, but in many cases is as high as 25, and in one case is 30. In the case of second chambers, eligibility for membership is even more demanding in terms of age: age requirements for taking seats are as low as 18 in 11 cases, 21 in a further 11, and 25 in 4 cases. But 14 second chambers have a minimum age of 30, 8 have 35 as a minimum, 4 prescribe 40 and one is limited to those aged 50 or more.

2.2.2 The term of office of members of the second chamber

In many cases the second chamber has the same term of office as the first chamber: four or five years are by far the most common terms. In some cases these are fixed terms, in others provision is made for premature dissolution. However, terms of two, three and six years also occur, and many second chambers – especially elected ones – are characterised by partial renewal. The position is summarised in table 3.

Table 3: Terms of office of members of second chambers, 1996

Term	Unitary states	Federal states	Total
2 years	0	1	1
3 years	1	1	2
4 years	11	2	13
4 years (half renewed every 2 years)	1	0	1
5 years	16	2	18
6 years	2	0	2
6 years (half renewed every 3 years)	4	3	7
6 years (third renewed every 2 years)	2	3	5
8 years (half renewed every 4 years)	1	1	2
9 years (third renewed every 3 years)	1	0	1
term fixed by local units	0	4	4
term not fixed	1	1	2
Total	40	18	58

Note: In the case of those chambers which make provision for full renewal, the terms above may be either fixed or (if there is provision for premature dissolution) maximum

Source: computed from sources cited in annexe 1

It will be seen that when senators have a term of six years, the chamber is normally renewed in stages: either one-third retire every two years, or half retire every three years. When the term is longer than this, partial renewal is always provided for. In a number of cases, members of second chambers have an indefinite term of office: for life, normally, in the British House of Lords, and until the age of seventy-five in the Canadian senate. In certain federal states, the term of office is laid down by the component units of the federation rather than by the constitution: Austria, Germany, the Russian Federation and Switzerland are examples.

2.2.3 The size of the second chamber

The size of the second house of parliament has been a matter of debate in many societies including Ireland. This is typically assessed against two criteria: the overall size of the population in the country in question (the argument being that small countries do not need or cannot afford a large second chamber), and the size of the first chamber, which is typically considerably larger than the second chamber, reflecting the more central role that it normally plays in the political process.

In general, second chambers are larger in countries with larger populations. Table 4 shows the relationship between the size of the upper house and the population of the country in which it is to be found. The strength of the relationship is obvious, though the presence of the British House of Lords in the second category distorts the picture a little. When we move to the third category (countries with a population of between one and 10 million), which includes Ireland, we can see that second chambers range in size from 15 to 70 members with 42 as the mean, or average, size.

Table 4: Size of second chamber related to population, 1996

Population band	Size of second chamber				
	Smallest	Largest	Mean	Median	Number
More than 100 million	81	252	157	139	6
10-99 million	24	1,191	161	90	25
1-9 million	15	70	42	37	18
Less than 1 million	8	34	18	16	9
Total	8	1,191	101	60	58

Note: the population data relate to 1994
Source: computed from sources cited in annexe 1

The relationship between the size of the two legislative chambers also needs to be considered. The second chamber is normally smaller than the first – in some cases, much smaller. This is frequently the case in federal states where the second chamber has clearly defined powers that are independent of its size (where, for example, the second chamber cannot simply be outvoted in a joint sitting of the two houses). In these circumstances, the size of the second chamber may have been defined originally in terms of the number of representatives assigned to each of the component units of the federation (for example, two in the case of Switzerland and the United States). The lower house, however, has been left free to expand, and this process has frequently been associated with population growth. This tendency towards relatively small second chambers in federal states is clear from table 5, which shows that all federal second chambers are less than 60% of the size of the corresponding first chambers.[26] Table 5 also shows that Ireland, with 36% as many senators as TDs, is very much part of the mainstream in this regard.

---

[26] The largest federal second chamber, in relation to the size of the lower house, is the Australian senate (51% of the size of the latter); the median ratio for federal chambers is 32% and for unitary ones 50%

Table 5: Size of second chamber in relation to size of first chamber, 1996

Second chamber as % of size of first chamber	Unitary states	Federal states	Total
More than 100%	3	0	3
80-99% of size	4	0	4
60-79%	7	0	7
40-59%	12	5	17
20-39%	13	11	24
Less than 20%	1	2	3
Total	40	18	58

Note: The ratio of members of the second chamber to members of the first ranges from 10% to 200% in unitary states and from 10% to 51% in federal states

Source: computed from sources cited in annexe 1

In a very small number of cases we find that, for peculiar local reasons, the second chamber is much larger than the first. This is the case in three countries. First, in the United Kingdom the House of Lords has gradually expanded to an enormous size – well over a thousand, at least nominally. Since most of its members are hereditary peers, many of whom belong to the families of persons ennobled in the distant past whose descendants no longer have much interest in political affairs, the effective size of the House of Lords is much smaller.[27] In Kyrghyzstan a peculiar relationship exists between the two houses of parliament: the House of Representatives and the Legislative Assembly are both directly elected for a five-year term by identical means, using the majority system; the former, with 70 members, is double the size of the latter, but it meets infrequently and because of its lesser role it is seen as a second chamber. In Burkina Faso, the directly elected Chamber of People's Deputies, with 107 members, is smaller than the appointed House of Representatives, with 178 members, which despite its name similarly fills the role of a second chamber.

2.3 Powers

Taking as our starting point the traditional separation of powers between legislature, executive and judiciary, we typically find that the second chamber has a subordinate role in each. In the legislative process, its power to veto legislation is normally suspensive rather than absolute. Most legislation is introduced and goes through its formative stages in the lower house and the second chamber's smaller size tends to give it less influence in joint committees or collective meetings of the two houses. It normally lacks

---

[27] During the parliamentary session 1995-96, for instance, only 457 peers attended one third of the sittings or more (hereditary members formed a minority of this group), while a further 415 were present for at least one sitting (United Kingdom: House of Lords, 1996). See also the discussion in Carnarvon et al, 1995

the power to appoint and dismiss members of the executive, and its capacity to review the work of the government is typically limited. In the judicial area, the first chamber is normally the one that makes appointments or has a controlling influence on these.

Nevertheless, there may be important areas in which the upper house has considerable power – more, perhaps, than the lower house. In many cases it may have a special role to play in the legislative process – equal to or even greater than that of the lower house, as in the case of the United States senate in the arena of foreign policy. It may also share with the lower house the right to make or break governments (as in Italy), or it may have a special relationship with the executive, as in the case, of the United States, where the senate can review the president's cabinet and other appointments and where the vice president is ex officio president of the senate. It may have been given special functions in judicial matters. For example, a senate may in many cases act as a tribunal of enquiry, or it may even have a clearly defined superior judicial function, as in the case of the British House of Lords. In many cases the second chamber is given honorary priority over the first: it is listed first in state lists, and its president takes precedence over the president of the lower house in the state hierarchy. Greater prestige may also attach to membership of the second chamber, not just because of the status of that body but because when it is both small and directly elected its members may represent a much larger section of the population and hold office for a longer term than members of the lower house.

We have tried in annexe 2 to review the relative power of second chambers in western Europe. This power tends to be most extensive in the legislative domain, where second chambers such as the Italian senate have a range of powers equal to that of the lower house. More often, however, the capacity of the second chamber is restricted, and this is especially the case in financial matters and in constitutional reform. In these areas the capacity of the second chamber to initiate or amend legislation tends to be limited. In general, too, the second chamber's veto on legislation is suspensive only – for approximately a year in the British House of Lords, or two months in Austria and Spain. In the executive field, the second chamber generally plays no role in appointing and dismissing governments, although again there are exceptions such as Italy. However, it may play a major role in reviewing the conduct of the executive, though in cases such as Ireland the role is minimal. The authority of the second chamber tends to be greater, other things being equal, in those cases where it cannot be dissolved by the government, as in Britain and the federal states considered here.[28]

Although it is difficult to quantify the relative power of the two houses, we have attempted to do so in table 6, using a crude conventional assessment of the power of the second chamber vis-a-vis the first, based on the criteria discussed above. Not surprisingly, the second chamber appears to have a rather more powerful role in federal states than in unitary ones. In the case of

---

[28] These remarks are based on the comparative studies included in the major collection of essays on European second chambers, Mastias and Grangé, 1987

the United States, the senate is conventionally seen as the more powerful of the two chambers, while the small House of Peoples in Bosnia-Herzegovina has been given a similarly influential role. But there are many second chambers of unitary states which are, at least technically and constitutionally, of equal importance to the first chamber (in Italy and Uruguay, for example), while in certain federal states (such as Austria and Germany) the federal councils are of lesser importance.

Table 6: Power of second chamber in relation to power of first chamber, 1996

Power of second chamber in relation to first chamber	Unitary states	Federal states	Total
Greater	0	2	2
More or less equal	9	6	15
Less	31	10	41
Total	40	18	58

Source: computed from sources cited in annexe 1

Table 7: Power of second chamber in relation to power of first chamber, by selection principle, 1996

Dominant principle of selection	Power of second chamber	Unitary states	Federal states	Total
Direct election	high	7	6	13
	low	9	2	11
Indirect election	high	0	2	2
	low	7	6	13
Appointment	high	2	0	2
	low	11	2	13
Other	high	0	0	0
	low	4	0	4
Total	high	9	8	17
	low	31	10	41
	total	40	18	58

Note: In assessing the power of the second chamber, those whose powers are greater than or approximately equal to the powers of the lower house have been classified as 'high', others as 'low'

Source: computed from sources cited in annexe 1

The relative power of the second chamber does appear to be related to the principle of selection. As we can see from table 7, directly elected chambers tend to be rather more powerful than those selected by some other principle, regardless of the question whether the state is a unitary or a federal one. Thus 13 out of 24 directly elected chambers (most of them in unitary states) have powers equal to or greater than the lower house, but the corresponding figures for indirectly elected chambers are 2 out of 15, and for appointed houses exactly the same (again, 2 out of 15).

2.4 Concluding remarks

This comparative overview of the composition and powers of second chambers has set the position of Seanad Éireann in context. In terms of its composition, the Irish Senate is unique. We have to search hard, and below the level of national parliaments, to find any second chamber with the vocational principle as its primary basis of composition; and the manner of selection of 'vocational' senators in Ireland differs from the only other remotely comparable case, the senate of the Free State of Bavaria. The election of six senators by university graduates is similarly unusual. Finally, the appointment of eleven senators by the head of government in Ireland (rather than by the head of state, acting on the advice of the head of government) appears to be without parallel in contemporary national parliaments.

Similarities with other second chambers become more obvious when we examine the powers of Seanad Éireann. Its subordinate role in the legislative process and its restricted capacity to influence Money Bills and Bills to amend the constitution are comparable with most of its counterparts. Its weak position in relation to the government is, again, an echo of the limited capacity of second chambers in general to control or review the actions of the executive.

Finally, we should note that the political composition of second chambers quite frequently contrasts with that of the first, laying the groundwork for potential clashes between the two houses, but the process of government is not necessarily particularly unharmonious in consequence. We have assembled some comparative data in annexe 3, which shows that while in some cases governments routinely have huge majorities in both chambers, there are others where the party composition of the two can be sharply different. The Canadian senate and the British House of Lords are two examples of such potential conflicts: the composition of the upper house remains predictable and stable, while that of the other chamber may lurch from one political extreme to the other.

3   THE ROLE OF SEANAD ÉIREANN

We consider the role played by Seanad Éireann in the political life of the state by first looking at the evolution of the current institutional arrangements; we go on to examine, second, the composition and, third, the powers of the Seanad.

3.1 Evolution of the Seanad

Bicameralism has almost always been an integral part of the Irish parliamentary tradition. The old Irish parliament that first met in Castledermot, Co Kildare, in 1264 evolved over time into a tricameral body similar to other medieval parliaments. There was a house of lords (including the lords spiritual and temporal), a house of commons (including representatives of knights of the shires, citizens of cities and burgesses of boroughs) and a house of clerical proctors (including representatives of the lower clergy). With the abolition of the third chamber in 1536, following its opposition to reformation legislation, the Irish parliament came to resemble its English, and later British, counterpart (Bradshaw, 1973: 74). Following the merger of the British and Irish parliaments in 1800, elections to the lower house were steadily democratised. By 1884 legal differences in parliamentary representation between cities, boroughs and shires, as well as between Ireland and other parts of the United Kingdom, had substantially disappeared. Ireland continued, however, to be represented in the British upper house by twenty-eight peers elected by the Irish peerage and by four Protestant bishops or archbishops.

Perhaps because of the strength of this tradition within the sphere of British political and cultural influence, but also undoubtedly because of circumstances peculiar to Ireland, all 'home rule' legislation proposing the establishment of a separate Irish legislature involved bicameral arrangements. Thus the Government of Ireland (Home Rule) Bill of 1886, defeated in the House of Commons, proposed that, in addition to a popularly-elected Second Order of 204 members, there would be a First Order, or upper house, of 103 members (75 elected for a 10-year period by voters with a high property qualification, and 28 representatives of the Irish peerage). The Government of Ireland (Home Rule) of 1893, which was passed by the House of Commons but defeated in the House of Lords, proposed that alongside a popularly elected Assembly of 103 members there would be a Council or upper chamber of 48, elected for an eight-year term by electors with a high property qualification. The Government of Ireland Bill of 1912, enacted notwithstanding a suspensive veto in the House of Lords as the Government of Ireland Act of 1914, made similar provision for a popularly elected House of Commons with 164 members and a Senate with 40; senators were initially to be nominated by the Lord Lieutenant, but would later be elected for a five-year term under the existing franchise.[29]

It was the latter piece of legislation that laid the basis for bicameralism in independent Ireland. The replacement of the 1914 act by the Government of Ireland Act of 1920 was marked by the introduction of partition and the installation of parallel parliamentary institutions in Dublin and Belfast. The act proposed that, alongside the Houses of Commons of Southern Ireland (with 128 members) and Northern Ireland (with 52), there would be a Senate

---

[29] Senators were to be elected from the four provinces by the single transferable vote system of proportional representation (14 from Ulster, 11 from Leinster, 9 from Munster and 6 from Connacht)

of Southern Ireland (with 64 members) and of Northern Ireland (with 26). The latter body, which survived until 1972, consisted of the lord mayor of Belfast and the mayor of Derry as ex officio members, with 24 members elected by the House of Commons for an eight-year term, one-half retiring every four years. The Senate of Southern Ireland had a more complex composition, one that was especially interesting in the light of later notions of corporate representation. Its make-up was as follows (and was subject to a residence requirement on the part of senators elected to represent particular groups and of those electing them):[30]

- 3 ex officio members (the lord chancellor and the lord mayors of Dublin and Cork)

- 17 members nominated by the lord lieutenant to represent commerce (including banking), labour and the scientific and learned professions

- 4 Catholic bishops, elected by the Catholic bishops

- 2 Church of Ireland bishops, elected by the Church of Ireland bishops

- 16 peers, elected by the Irish peerage

- 8 privy councillors, elected by the Irish Privy Council

- 14 county or county borough councillors, elected on a provincial basis (4 each from Leinster, Munster and Connacht and 2 from the three Ulster counties).

This body met on only two occasions; its legitimacy was seriously undermined by the fact that Sinn Féin won 124 of the 128 seats in the House of Commons and simply refused to work with the institutions of 'Southern Ireland'.[31] Nevertheless, the notion of a second chamber was retained in the Anglo-Irish treaty of 1921 and in the settlement arrived at between the new Irish government and representatives of the southern unionists.

The 60-member Senate established in the 1922 Constitution was to be directly elected for a 12-year period, one-quarter of the senators retiring every three years. However, candidates were to be nominated by the Dáil and the Seanad 'on the grounds that they have done honour to the Nation by reason of useful public service or that, because of special qualifications or attainments, they represent important aspects of the Nation's life'.[32] This was an oblique but not necessarily effective mechanism for complying with a commitment that the southern Protestant minority would receive adequate

---

[30] They were required to be resident within the Irish Free State, or, in the case of the bishops and archbishops, to have dioceses extending into that territory

[31] Sinn Féin adopted the interpretation that the 1921 elections to the houses of commons of Southern Ireland and Northern Ireland were elections to the second Dáil

[32] See Köhn, 1932: 190-195; the discussions and the agreement between the southern unionists and the government that led to this arrangement are reported in detail in Buckland, 1972: 318-324

representation in the second chamber. As a special transitional measure, the first Senate in 1922 was partly elected by the Dáil (30 senators) and partly appointed by the President of the Executive Council, WT Cosgrave (30 senators).

The first triennial popular election took place in 1925. Because of casual vacancies, the number of places to be filled had increased from 15 to 19, and these were to be elected by a general vote of all those aged 30 or more, by means of the single transferable vote system of proportional representation, with the whole territory of the Irish Free State as a single constituency. There were 76 candidates, and 67 counts were required to complete the electoral process. Although only 24% of the electorate had voted, the counting of the votes took three weeks to complete. When the next triennial elections fell due in 1928 the system was changed: the term of senators was reduced to nine years, one third of whom were to retire every three years, and the general electorate was abolished, to be replaced by an electoral college consisting of Dáil deputies and existing senators.

Notwithstanding the successive changes made in its composition, the Senate of the Irish Free State left a creditable legislative record. If this is measured in terms of amendments made to Bills, the raw figures are high. In all, amendments affected 37% of Bills during the life of the first Senate (1922-36), and eight Bills were rejected, of which two were subsequently dropped by the government. As a standard of comparison, during the lifetime of the Seanad (from 1938 to 19 September 1995) 18% of Bills were amended, but Bills were rejected outright on only one occasion.[33] (Under existing constitutional arrangements, the disputed measure was subsequently passed.) The historian of the first Senate, like many others, paid tribute to its major role as a forum for debate.[34]

One feature of the first Irish Senate was that its political composition contrasted sharply with that of the Dáil. Of its initial members, only 36 out of 60 were Catholics, and the landed gentry and the ex-unionist community were strongly represented. This was reflected in the fact that the first Cathaoirleach of the Seanad, Lord Glenavy, had been a prominent unionist and supporter of Edward Carson. But this pattern of composition, and the slow pace at which it changed, also planted the seeds for serious conflict with the lower house. Disagreements between the houses were of little political significance while the pro-Treaty Cumann na nGaedheal government held office up to 1932, but after that clashes with the Dáil became more serious in their implications, as de Valera sought to effect fundamental changes in the Constitution of the state.[35] The long-term

---

[33] This was the Third Amendment of the Constitution Bill 1958

[34] See O'Sullivan, 1940; for other tributes to the work of the first senate see, for instance, Dooge 1987

[35] Formally organised parties developed only slowly in the Senate in the 1920s. A pro-Cumann na nGaedheal 'Progressive Party' was formed in the late 1920s, but was replaced by a formally organised Cumann na nGaedheal group, which had 19 members after the 1928 election (rising to 21 in 1931 and 22 in 1934); Fianna

consequence was the abolition of the senate in 1936, and the introduction of a brief period of unicameralism.

Scarcely had the Senate been abolished, however, than the government began to consider mechanisms for its replacement in the new Constitution then being drafted. A commission was appointed to examine the powers and composition of a second chamber, should one be established. The commission recommended that any new senate should have powers similar to the old one (though with a reduced capacity to delay legislation); that its life span should coincide with that of the Dáil; and that it should consist of 45 members, of whom 15 would be nominated by the President of the Executive Council and 30 would be elected from a panel drawn up by a nominating authority elected by the Dáil. In the case of elected members, it proposed that nominations should, as far as practicable, have regard to specific public interests and services,[36] and that these 30 members should be elected by an electoral college consisting of all candidates at the previous Dáil election. An important minority report, which had more influence on the subsequent shape of the Constitution than the report of the majority, recommended a slightly different schema. It proposed a 50-member second chamber whose duration would be linked to that of the Dáil, with 10 members nominated by the President of the Executive Council, specifically to represent four designated areas,[37] and 40 members elected by the Dáil from four panels of candidates put forward by various vocational or functional interests: farming and fisheries, labour, industry and commerce, and education and the learned professions (Second House of the Oireachtas Commission, 1936).

The new constitution of 1937 reintroduced a second chamber, following the broad lines of the minority report of the Commission on the Second Chamber. The number of nominated members was increased to 11, and the number of vocational members to 49, with the addition of a fifth panel, public administration. Apart from specifying the minimum and maximum size of each panel (none was to have fewer than 5 or more than 11 members), the constitution provided that 6 of the vocational members be elected by graduates of the two existing universities, but otherwise left open the system of nomination and election.[38]

Fáil had 7 seats after the 1928 (rising to 13 in 1931 and 19 in 1935), while the Labour Party had 6 senators in 1928 and 1931 (rising to 7 in 1934) (O'Sullivan 1940: 447)

[36] These were national language and culture; the arts; agriculture and fisheries; industry and commerce; finance; health and social welfare; foreign affairs; education; law; labour; and public administration

[37] These were national language and culture (three nominees), public administration, economics or foreign affairs (four), public health and social services (two) and literature and the fine arts (one)

[38] For general discussion of Seanad Éireann, see Garvin, 1969; Smyth, 1972; and Grangé, 1987. Seanad elections are discussed in Manning, 1978; Coakley, 1980; 1987; 1990; 1993

It was, then, the original intention of the 1937 Constitution that these members would represent so-called 'vocational' interests. This view derived from Catholic social teaching, and more specifically from the encyclical *Quadragesimo Anno* of Pope Pius XI (1931). This had stressed, as an alternative to class conflict, an institutionalisation of sectoral divisions based essentially on groupings of occupations and of other major social interests. As the encyclical put it:

> True and genuine social order demands that the various members of a society be joined together by some firm bond. Such a bond of union is provided both by the production of goods or the rendering of services in which employers and employees of one and the same vocational group collaborate; and by the common good which all such groups should unite to promote, each in its own sphere, with friendly harmony.[39]

Experimentation with vocational representation at the time that the Constitution was drawn up was most developed in Italy and Portugal, but the 1937 Constitution was rather half-hearted in following the lead of these countries. It identified five groups of 'interests and services' that were to be represented in the second chamber, each of them by a minimum of five and a maximum of eleven senators (these were the five areas mentioned above; see further discussion in section 3.3 below). Those elected were to have 'knowledge and practical experience' of the sector with which they were associated, but the Constitution was otherwise silent on the manner of election.

The Seanad Electoral (Panel Members) Act 1937, which sought to give flesh to these provisions, introduced some features that have persisted to the present. First, it fixed the number of members allocated to each panel at the figure at which it remains today. Second, it provided for an extremely complicated system of candidate nomination that distinguished between (1) a subpanel of candidates proposed by special 'nominating bodies' authorised to put forward names and (2) a subpanel of candidates proposed by parliamentarians. Third, it provided for an electorate to consist of a mixture of parliamentarians and local councillors. Early difficulties with the implementation of the act led to minor changes in the system of nomination and to major changes in the system of election.

The biggest problem with the original system of election was that the electoral quota (the number of votes needed for election) was so low that it encouraged electoral abuses and there were allegations of bribery and vote-buying. All 43 panel seats were to be filled as if they were part of a single constituency, and the electorate was relatively low (it consisted of newly-elected members of the Dáil and 7 representatives from each county and county borough council). In the first senate election in 1938, for instance, the total electorate comprised 354 people, of whom 330 voted.[40] This meant that the electoral quota amounted to a little over 8 votes. The Seanad Electoral

---

[39] Cited in Commission on Vocational Organisation, 1943: 8

[40] *Irish Times*, 29 March 1938

(Panel Members) Act 1947, provided, however, for 5 separate elections, one for each panel, and extended the electorate to include all members of county and county borough councils, as well as outgoing senators. Minor changes were made by the Seanad Electoral (Panel Members) Act 1954, whose main effect was to abolish the 'nomination committees' established by the 1947 act to review candidates in each of the five panels.

Seanad Éireann has survived in this manner to the present. This is notwithstanding a number of enquiries into its composition, several of which incorporated criticism of the manner in which the system of vocational representation was operating. These began with the report of a special committee of the Dáil in 1937 on the Seanad Electoral Bill and were continued by a joint committee on Seanad panel elections in 1947, a select committee on the Seanad Electoral (Panel Members) Bill in 1952 and the Seanad Electoral Law Commission Report of 1959. In addition, the composition of the Seanad was analysed critically by the Commission on Vocational Organisation (1943: 309), which dismissed the idea that it could be seen as a vocational assembly, and, less harshly, by the Committee on the Constitution (1967: 29).[41]

3.2 Current composition of the Seanad

What is important about the composition of any senate is 'to take account of political interests that may not be adequately represented in the main house', and to ensure that 'the composition of the upper house does not simply mirror that of the lower house'. In short, '[a] fundamental justification for the existence of a second house is that it differs from the main house in its representative character.' (Constitution Review Group, 1996a: 68).

In Ireland, just as in many other European countries, tight party discipline, exercised via the whip system, means that the government retains firm control of the legislative process in the lower house. If the composition of the upper house precisely mirrors the party system in the lower house, then no real checks or balances can be applied by the upper house. What can be forced summarily through the lower house can be forced in exactly the same way through the upper. In this event, the upper house serves no real purpose. Its other functions, such as providing detailed scrutiny of the wording of Bills, or providing members for legislative committees, can more effectively be fulfilled by improved structures within the lower house. This is why a fundamental justification for the existence of an upper house is that its composition differs from that of the lower house. If it does not so differ in a world of tight party discipline – a world, we should note, never envisaged explicitly in the 1937 Constitution – then the upper house is merely a political extension of the lower, and might as well be merged with it.

---

[41] See Dáil Éireann, 1937; Oireachtas Éireann, 1947; Seanad Éireann, 1953; Seanad Electoral Law Commission, 1959. Other related reports included that of the joint committee on the constitution of the Seanad (Oireachtas Éireann, 1928) and an inter-departmental committee on Seanad electoral law that reported in 1951

So how can we evaluate the composition of Seanad Éireann in this regard? Those merely reading the wording of Articles 18 and 19 of the Constitution might be forgiven for thinking that the composition of Seanad Éireann differed very radically indeed from that of the lower house, the Dáil. Indeed the differences might appear to be far more fundamental than those in almost any other parliamentary democracy. As we have just seen, the Constitution appears to provide for a Seanad drawn from *vocational* constituencies, as opposed to the *geographical* constituencies that form the basis of representation in virtually every other modern legislature.

These vocational constituencies include university graduates, as well as 'panels' set out in Article 18.7.1°, representing:

- national language and culture, literature, art, education ...

- agriculture and allied interests, and fisheries

- labour, whether organised or unorganised

- industry and commerce, including banking, finance, accountancy, engineering and architecture

- public administration and social services, including voluntary social activities.

The vocational constituencies listed above, furthermore, were not intended to be enshrined in the Constitution for all time since, according to Article 19, '[p]rovision may be made by law *for the direct election by any functional or vocational group* or association or council of so many members of Seanad Éireann as may be fixed by such law in substitution for an equal number of the members to be elected from the corresponding panels ...' (emphasis added).

To the vocational constituencies were added 11 members nominated by the Taoiseach, a provision in theory intended to give the opportunity to represent voices that would not otherwise be heard in the Oireachtas. The 1937 Constitution, therefore, sets out a framework for a Seanad that is radically different from the norm in most western democracies, a Seanad composed on vocational lines that on the face of things looks most unlikely to mirror the composition of the lower house.

The reality, as everyone who knows anything about Irish politics will be aware, is quite different. This situation has arisen as a result of the precise system of nomination and election to the 'vocational' panels, a matter left by Article 18.10.1° to be regulated by law. The legislation that has emerged to regulate nomination and election to Seanad Éireann, outlined in the previous section, is complex and obscure for a body that has rather little de facto power (see discussions in Casey, 1992: 98-101; Kelly, 1994: 181-83; Morgan, 1990: 185-88).

The key point about this process is that, while nominations for panel members originate either from members of the Oireachtas or from vocational 'nominating bodies', and while the law does provide that candidates shall satisfy the returning officer that they have knowledge and practical experience in the 'interests or services' of the vocational panel in question, this requirement has been interpreted very liberally. In the one case on the matter dealt with by the High Court (discussed in Kelly, 1994: 183), it was explicitly noted that the Constitution does not require *special* knowledge or practical experience of matters relating to a vocational panel, and is furthermore silent on how such knowledge and experience might have been gained.

Nomination and election procedures cannot be considered in isolation from each other, however, since these obviously interact in their practical effect. In any political system, candidates who have little chance of being elected obviously have much less chance of being nominated in the first place than those who are expected to be more successful in the eventual election. This means that probably the most important factor conditioning the composition of Seanad Éireann is the composition of the electorate for the panel members. This electorate is very limited and very party political, comprising 166 members of the lower house (TDs), and up to 60 outgoing senators, together with members of county and county borough councils, normally generating an electorate of between 900 and 1,000 people. The great majority of these are politicians affiliated to one of the main political parties in the Dáil, as is clear from table 8, which summarises the political composition of the Seanad electorate at a range of recent points in time. This means, as Casey (1992: 99-100) observes, that 'in reality the Seanad electoral process is dominated by party politics. Nowadays even some of the university senators have overt party affiliations. The chances of being elected purely on vocational grounds are virtually nil.'[42]

Thus the vocational aspirations of the 1937 Constitution have been effectively confounded by subsequent legislative provisions for the nomination and election of senators, and the result has been an incorporation of the party politics of the Dáil into Seanad elections. This situation has been compounded by two further provisions in the Constitution that, given a partisan Seanad, render the upper house in Ireland effectively a creature of the lower. The first of these is the holding of Seanad elections 'not later than ninety days after a dissolution of Dáil Éireann' (Article 18.8), which in practice means a matter of weeks after a Dáil election. The second is the provision for the incoming Taoiseach, who will thus typically just have been installed in office as head of a single party or coalition government with a Dáil majority, to nominate 11 of the 60 new senators (Article 18.3).

---

[42] The partisan nature of Seanad elections since 1977, arising from the partisan composition of the panel electorate, has been documented in a series of studies of these elections; see Coakley 1980; 1987; 1990; 1993

Table 8: Approximate political composition of the Seanad panel electorate, 1977, 1981, 1989 and 1993

Year	Fianna Fáil	Fine Gael	Labour	Others	Total
1977	379 (43.7)	307 (35.4)	90 (10.4)	92 (10.6)	868 (100.0)
1981	404 (44.7)	335 (37.1)	82 (9.1)	82 (9.1)	903 (100.0)
1989	463 (48.0)	298 (31.0)	59 (6.2)	136 (14.9)	956 (100.0)
1993	404 (41.9)	289 (29.9)	93 (9.6)	179 (18.5)	965 (100.0)

Source: Coakley 1980; 1987; 1990; 1993

These provisions combine to mean that, not only is a new Seanad partisan, but that it is almost certain to be dominated by an incoming government that must itself have commanded a Dáil majority for the Taoiseach to have been installed. While the partisan balance of the outgoing senators and the existing county councillors may reflect the political vagaries of elections held in previous years, the partisan balance of the incoming TDs, and above all the new Taoiseach's right to make 11 nominations out of a total of 60 senators, combine to ensure that the government party or parties can normally expect to control a secure majority in the Seanad.

The only exception to this rule is the situation that arose in 1994 when, for the first time in the history of the state, a government with a new partisan composition was formed without a dissolution of the Dáil and the holding of a general election. The result was that the new Taoiseach did not have a right to nominate new senators, and the new government did not have a secure partisan majority in what was essentially the 'old' upper house.

In a very real sense, however, the 1994-97 situation is an exceptional one that highlights the main critique of the composition of the current Seanad, which can be characterised in one of two ways. Either the Seanad is dominated by precisely the same partisan forces that control the Dáil, by virtue of the very partisan composition of the Seanad electorate, the fact that Seanad elections must follow Dáil elections, and the Taoiseach's 11 nominees. Or, as may be the case if the government changes without a dissolution of the Dáil, the Seanad is dominated by the partisan forces that put the *previous* government into office. In the latter case, the new Taoiseach must live with a partisan Seanad in which the balance of forces is determined by the defeated Taoiseach's 11 nominees. This is a clearly unintended situation in which an outgoing government that has presumably lost power as a result of some political failure or another casts a very long shadow over the government that has replaced it.

In short, the bottom line of this discussion is a two-pronged critique of the composition of Seanad Éireann as it is currently constituted. Either the balance of partisan forces in the Seanad mirrors that in the Dáil, which undermines the rationale for having a Seanad in the first place; or it reflects the partisan forces that put the previous government in place, which would appear to be a perverse, unintended and not particularly defensible way for the composition of an upper house to differ from that of the lower.

3.3 Current powers of the Seanad

The theoretical position of the Seanad in the system of checks and balances in Ireland derives from its role in the *legislative* process, explicitly set out in Articles 20-24 of the Constitution,[43] combined with an as yet unused provision in Article 27 for triggering a popular referendum or general election on Bills 'of national importance'. The Seanad plays no part at all in the choice of an *executive*, a matter which is arguably the most important function of the Dáil, as it is of the lower house in any parliamentary democracy. A new Taoiseach is effectively voted into office by the Dáil. An incumbent Taoiseach can be put out of office by losing the confidence of the Dáil. Furthermore, rather than the Seanad having any impact on the composition of the government, it is currently the government, as we saw in the previous section, that has an impact on the composition of the Seanad.

In relation to the Seanad's role in the legislative process, Casey (1992: 101) clearly summarises the position. '[T]he Constitution makes it clear that the ultimate power lies with the Dáil. Articles 20-24 put this beyond any doubt. They show that the Seanad's only power over legislation is to delay it – and for a relatively brief period only. Moreover, its authority in the financial field is severely limited.'

Under Articles 20-24, the Seanad has 21 days to deal with a 'money' Bill, which it cannot initiate or amend, and on which it is confined to making recommendations that the Dáil is free to ignore. After 21 days, the Dáil can deem any money Bill to have been passed, regardless of anything that has happened in the Seanad (Article 21.2.2°). For non-money Bills, the Seanad's time for consideration is a 'stated period' of 90 days (Article 23.1.1°-2°), after which the Dáil can refuse to accept any Seanad amendments and can by resolution deem the Bill to have been passed. The net effect of these provisions is that the Seanad, if it disagrees with the Dáil, can delay a money Bill by at most 21 days, and a non-money Bill by at most 90 days. These are hardly earth-shattering powers.

The severely abridged power of the Seanad to have any input into money Bills clearly reflects a view that the upper house should not interfere with matters, such as the budget, that have to do with the essential good

---

[43] Note that there are technical flaws in the Constitution's description of this procedure, discussed by Casey (1992: 103-104) and Kelly (1994: 193-194), but that these do not impinge upon the more general arguments we are dealing with here

government of the country. Since the Seanad has no role in choosing and supporting the government, it is clearly arguable that it should have no role in how the government runs the country, a role that it would indeed have if it were given any real power to block the government's budget.

The argument in relation to non-money legislation, however, is less clear cut. It might be claimed that all legislation is fundamentally a matter for the government of the day but, whatever about the political practice arising from firm party discipline and tight government control of the legislative process, this is certainly not the constitutional theory. What, after all, is the upper house of a legislature to deliberate about if it is not to deliberate about legislation? And what does that deliberation mean if, when the chips are down, it can be utterly ignored by the lower house?

These questions bring us to the heart of a dilemma that anyone with an interest in the future of Seanad Éireann must resolve. If we feel the need for a second chamber, then we must feel that the second chamber has something useful to do. How can it have something useful to do if it can always be overruled by the first chamber? But how do we resolve the deadlocks on vital issues that will surely arise from time to time if it cannot always be overruled by the first chamber?

There is no easy constitutional resolution to this dilemma, although the 90-day delay period written into the Constitution is perhaps intended to resolve it at the level of practical politics. In effect, the Seanad has some modest power of delay and debate with which to annoy the Dáil and the government, and in this way perhaps to force them, in anticipation, to take account of the views of the Seanad. To the extent to which debate in the Seanad is publicised and taken seriously, Seanad opposition may turn up the pressure of public opinion on the Dáil and the government. To the extent to which time is of the essence in legislation, the threat of a 90-day delay may be a sufficient annoyance for the Dáil and the government to try and avoid this by taking the views of the Seanad on board.

There are two essential practical problems with this argument. The first is that time is rarely so much of the essence of legislation that a 90-day delay is any real threat as the biggest stick with which the Seanad can beat the Dáil. But the big practical problem derives from the very composition of the Seanad that we discussed in the previous section. Since partisan control over the Seanad mirrors that over the Dáil, the two houses very rarely come into conflict. The result is that, not only is the limited power of delay rarely used in earnest, but debate in the Seanad is perceived by the public as a rehash of Dáil party politics and has little real impact on public opinion. Even the limited 90-day delay period might have a more important effect if the composition of the Seanad routinely differed from that of the Dáil; but in practice it does not. It all hardly seems to be sufficient justification for an entire second chamber of the legislature.

The Seanad does have another power, however; the possibility of triggering an Article 27 referendum or general election. Under Article 27.1, a majority of the Seanad, combined with one-third of the members of the Dáil, may petition the President that a Bill 'contains a proposal of such national importance that the will of the people thereon ought to be ascertained'. The President must consult the Council of State but has absolute discretion in the matter. If the President accedes to the petition, then the will of the people must be ascertained either by a referendum or by dissolving the Dáil and having a general election (Article 27.5).

This apparently considerable power has never been used, presumably because of the traditional control of the Seanad by the government, arising for all of the reasons that we have already discussed. But, if the partisan majority in the Seanad did differ from that in the Dáil in such a way that an opposition in the Dáil controlled a majority in the Seanad, then the possibility arises that the Seanad, with the agreement of the President, could force either a referendum or a general election on a Bill containing matter of 'national importance'. Once more we see that de jure powers might well take on quite a different de facto significance if the composition of the Seanad no longer habitually mirrored that of the Dáil.

Two other roles fulfilled by the Seanad, quite apart from its role as part of the checks and balances in the legislative system, are to provide a source of members for legislative committees, and to be able if called upon to provide up to two members of the cabinet and possibly a number of ministers of state. Both roles are potentially quite important in the political system as a whole, though neither is quintessentially a matter for an upper house of the legislature.

The Irish Constitution, like the constitutions of other English-speaking parliamentary democracies, requires that members of the government also be members of the legislature. In continental Europe, by contrast, there is no such requirement, and it is common for people other than legislators to be members of the government. Indeed, in certain countries such as France, the Netherlands and Norway, government ministers are prohibited from being members of parliament, and any parliamentarians appointed to the government must resign their seats. In a small country such as Ireland, the requirement of parliamentary membership is quite demanding. To begin with, it takes more than 30 senior politicians from whichever party or parties are in government, typically with little more than 80 Dáil seats, to fill the vital jobs of cabinet ministers, junior ministers and government whips. Add a share of key committee chairs to the roster of important jobs and subtract those TDs who are unavailable for such appointments (whether for political, personal or professional reasons) and it is clear that the list of able and available appointees on the government side is inevitably going to be spread pretty thinly. On top of this, a range of important legislative committees must be staffed. Without the Seanad to supply talent for the committee system, the current arrangements might well become unworkable. This, however, is a bonus for the committee system that is provided by the Seanad but, once more, supplying committee members cannot be seen as a fundamental rationale for having a second chamber. The same effect could be created by expanding the lower house, or by reforming the committee system.

The possibility that two members of the government may be members of the Seanad, combined with the Taoiseach's power to nominate senators, is the only way within the Irish Constitution in which a person who has been elected to neither house of the Oireachtas can become a cabinet minister. This power has been used only on two occasions since 1937 because in practice ministerial appointments are plum jobs that are jealously kept to themselves by TDs.[44] Even in theory, furthermore, there are more straightforward ways of finding a route into the cabinet for a talented but unelected individual than having as a conduit an entire second house of the legislature to which the head of government may nominate members.

3.4 Summarising the core critique of the Seanad

Overall, we can conclude that the fundamental role of a senate in a country such as Ireland is not making and breaking governments, not contributing to the staffing of the committee system, nor even providing the only route into the cabinet for the unelected. These important roles either are, or can be, fulfilled in other ways. The fundamental role of the Seanad, difficult to replace elsewhere in the system, is as an important part of the checks and balances that act as constraints on hasty and/or ill-considered legislation by the lower house.

It is in relation to this vital role that the current composition and powers of Seanad Éireann interact to generate a very strong argument for reform. It is not worth having an institution that makes no difference. To make a difference, an upper house must have some worthwhile powers over the legislative process, while its partisan composition must not mirror that of the lower house. The powers of the current Seanad – a 90-day delay of non-money Bills and a 21-day delay of money Bills – are very modest to start with. Some might say they are not worth the effort and cost of creating an entire second house of the legislature. But even these limited powers are effectively undermined by a system of representation that typically allows the government parties to run the affairs of the Seanad in precisely the same way that they run the affairs of the Dáil.

4   OPTIONS FOR CHANGE

The preceding discussion permits us to review the options for the future of Seanad Éireann by using comparative material on other second chambers and linking this with the history of bicameralism in Ireland and the discussion that has so far taken place on this subject. We do this by first making some general comments on the debate surrounding the Seanad and then going on to look at possible changes in the composition and powers of the second chamber. The first, and most stark, option is abolition, and we review in a separate subsection what might be involved if this were to happen. We then go on to look at various possibilities for reform. While these matters are in

---

[44] In 1957 Senator Sean Moylan and in 1982 Senator James Dooge were appointed to the government. Senator Joseph Connolly was a member of de Valera's government under the Free State Constitution

practice intimately linked with one another, for the sake of clarity we structure our discussion of the options in terms of possible reforms, first, of the composition of the Seanad and, second, of its powers. We conclude with some discussion of how reforms of both composition and powers might interact to generate possible blueprints for the future of Seanad Éireann.

4.1 Introduction: the debate

The future of any political institution is likely to be conditioned by its history: by the set of cultural values that gave rise to it in the first place, and by the impact that its very existence has had on these values.

It is notoriously difficult to assess what must always be the essentially subjective characteristics of a political culture. Yet we do have access to material submitted by the general public to commissions of enquiry into the Irish second chamber in the past, as well as to the deliberations of these commissions or committees and of the Dáil and Seanad themselves, when we attempt to assess opinion on this issue.

First, it seems to us that there is no strong body of opinion calling for the abolition of the Seanad. It is true that influential voices have called for its abolition, using economic or political arguments, but these have not formed part of any consistent and continuous campaign.[45] On the other hand, there is no evidence of a powerful lobby committed to the defence of the second chamber. Our impression is that mainstream opinion is tolerant of the Seanad rather than supportive of it: that it wishes to see the Seanad continue to exist, but that not many tears would necessarily be shed were it to be abolished. Of course, the position might change significantly if abolition were to become a matter of serious public debate.

Concerning opinions on the nature of the Seanad, and especially its composition, we can also come to some tentative conclusions. First, there appears to be little support for *direct election*. Comment on the only occasion on which the Seanad was directly elected, in 1925, has been overwhelmingly and strongly negative, and for many years this left a legacy of opposition to direct election. While we feel that much of the criticism of the 1925 experiment is badly informed, and that alternative and more effective systems of direct election could have been devised, we acknowledge that few voices have been raised since 1925 in defence of the principle of direct election.[46]

---

[45] The most consistent opposition came from the Progressive Democrats in their early years

[46] Examples of exceptions are Hugh Kennedy, chairman of the Second House of the Oireachtas Commission in 1936, who dissented from the report of his own commission and suggested that half of the Senate be directly elected from the four provinces, and Michael Laver, a member of the Constitution Review Group in 1996, who suggested that the Seanad be elected directly from large constituencies, possibly those used in elections to the European parliament. Both suggestions assumed a fixed term for the Seanad, independent of that of the Dáil

Neither does there appear to be much support for *indirect election* in the classical sense. Suggestions along these lines have been brought forward from time to time, but they have been few in number. Indeed, the Committee on the Constitution in 1967 rather trenchantly dismissed this option, on the grounds that:

> ... the political and historical reasons for this kind of representation in other countries have no relevance here and there would be no advantage for us in adopting this formula. Indeed, we would be inclined to feel that any arrangement that allocated senators on a geographical basis might, possibly, tend to create disharmony between different regions of the country (Committee on the Constitution 1967: 29-30).

While we do not share the above analysis, it is clear that there is little support for this principle of representation.

The idea of *election by the Dáil* appears to have attracted some support, especially in the past. A large portion of the Senate was elected in this way in 1922, and in 1928, 1931 and 1934 Dáil deputies made up the greater part of the electorate (existing senators comprising the remainder). The 1936 commission recommended that two-thirds of senators be elected by an electoral college consisting of all *candidates* in the previous Dáil election (of course, actual Dáil deputies would often have been outnumbered within this group too).[47] In the scheme finally approved, Dáil deputies were included as part of the electorate for the vocational panel seats, but they normally amount to about one-sixth of the total electorate. There has been little support for the idea of election of the Seanad by the Dáil since the 1930s. While it might have certain attractions to Dáil deputies themselves, there is little evidence that those without a vested interest in the matter would favour this principle.

The principle of *nomination* of at least a portion of the Seanad appears to be widely acceptable. Half of the members of the Seanad were nominated by the President of the Executive Council in 1922. The 1936 commission recommended that one-third be so nominated, while the dissenting report by its chairman recommended that half be nominated and the influential minority report recommended a nominate component of one-fifth.[48] In the final analysis the nominated proportion was less than one-fifth (11 out of 60 in the new Seanad). While submissions to later bodies on the issue of the composition of the Seanad have in some cases called for the abolition of this component, most have not.

---

[47] The numbers of candidates in the first four elections under the new Constitution, when the number of Dáil seats was 138, were 255 (1937), 214 (1938), 354 (1943) and 252 (1944) (Gallagher, 1993); the original Bunreacht na hÉireann Bill of 1937 had provided for an electorate consisting of all candidates winning at least 500 votes, but each elector's own vote in Seanad elections would be weighted according to his or her number of first preference votes

[48] One prominent member of the commission, Frank MacDermot, had earlier suggested that all of the members be nominated

In fact, the idea of a Seanad based on the *vocational principle* appears to have attracted the most widespread support. The government which drew up the Constitution that seeks to give expression to this principle within the present Seanad was, of course, a Fianna Fáil one. But the document on which the provisions for the Seanad were based, the minority report from the 1936 commission, was strongly influenced by Fine Gael; its signatories were certainly not noted as Fianna Fáil supporters. Furthermore, ideas on the corporatist restructuring of the state had been most extensively developed within Fine Gael (Manning, 1970: 217-231). But the original suggestion for a body composed on these lines came from the Labour Party during the course of the debate on the 1922 Constitution: it proposed a vocational second chamber, based on 14 groups.[49]

The actual implementation of provisions to give effect to the vocational principle attracted criticism almost from the outset. It quickly became clear that party political influence would outweigh vocational considerations in the selection of senators (see also the data in annexe 4). What was probably the consensus view was summarised by Basil Chubb in 1970, when he argued that '...the procedure of the house suffers from the fact that it is not composed on any basis that corresponds with the social structure of the community but is merely another selection of party politicians chosen in an unnecessarily complicated manner...' (Chubb 1970: 205). This view has frequently been echoed since then. Many alternatives to the present system have been discussed. Public submissions to the Seanad Electoral Law Commission in 1959 opted overwhelmingly for designation of senators by nominating bodies or, in a variant of this, election of senators from an electoral college consisting of nominating bodies only. Even among those accepting the existing electorate, there were many calls to the effect that only nominating bodies could put forward candidates, except possibly in the case of the administrative panel, where there was more tolerance of the possibility of candidacies proposed by members of the Oireachtas. In a few cases, there were proposals for the extension of the existing electorate (of members of the Oireachtas and local councillors): the possible addition of borough and urban district councillors or of representatives of nominating bodies, for instance, or the extension of the electorate to include all of those registered for jury service, or to all heads of families divided into vocational groups. The commission itself finally opted for a hybrid system: within each panel, some senators would be elected by nominating bodies from a list put forward by the same nominating bodies, while others would be elected by the existing electorate from a list put forward by members of the Oireachtas.

The recommendations of the commission were not implemented, and, in any case, the debate was constrained to follow existing constitutional provisions. Strikingly, however, the Committee on the Constitution in 1967, which was under no such constraint, supported the broad lines of the vocational approach, and submissions to the 1996 Constitution Review Group by and large continued in this mould (Constitution Review Group, 1996b: 134-143).

---

[49] See speech by Thomas Johnson, *Dáil debates*, vol 1, 4 October 1922, cols 1139-1142

As in 1959 there were proposals for giving the nominating bodies more influence and for broadening the electorate, and there were calls for the extension of representation to such groups as emigrants, travellers and the unemployed. Such attempts to redefine the existing system of vocational panels received their most developed expression in a proposal by one member of the Group, who proposed an alternative set of 11 panels that were essentially non-vocational.[50]

While acknowledging that the current political value system is likely to have a strong impact on any changes that are made to Seanad Éireann, it is important to remember the conclusions that emerge from our comparative study. While there are very many differences in the composition of second chambers, there are certain respects in which the Irish Senate is truly unique.

- *First,* the vocational principle has no parallel in the second chambers of other independent states, as we have already discussed at some length.

- *Second,* the idea of allowing six senators to be elected by university graduates (especially if this right is confined to the graduates of only two universities) is extremely unusual. It derives from the medieval idea of corporate representation, not from modern ideas of vocational representation (specifically, it derives from university representation in the old Irish and British parliaments, which was continued on after 1922 in Dáil Éireann and transferred to the Seanad in 1937). The 'university' senators, it should be emphasised, do not represent the universities; they represent university graduates, only a tiny proportion of whom are actually members of their universities.

- *Third,* appointment of a number of senators by the head of government rather than by the head of state is unique. This may well derive from a historical suspicion in Ireland of the head of state who, even in the early years of independent Ireland, was the British monarch, represented by the governor general. But the effect of giving the Taoiseach the right to nominate 11 senators amounts to giving the principal figure in the first chamber the right to nominate a sizeable proportion of the other chamber.

In the light of this overview of the debate, we may turn now to look at the options for a future Seanad Éireann in terms both of its composition and its powers, but beginning with the possibility of its outright abolition.

---

[50] See proposal by Dr Kathleen Lynch; the panels she suggested were (1) employer and farming sector (2) National Women's Council (3) Irish National Organisation of the Unemployed (4) trade unions (5) youth (6) older people (7) Northern Ireland (8) TDs and county councillors (9) minority groups, such as travellers (10) MEPs (11) emigrants. (Constitution Review Group, 1996b:529)

4.2 Abolition of the Seanad

The first thing to be said about the possibility of abolishing the Seanad is that there are many European states without a second chamber – Denmark, Finland, Greece, Iceland, Norway, Portugal and Sweden, for example. Furthermore, several second chambers have actually been abolished in the post-war parliamentary democracies – in Denmark, Sweden and New Zealand, for example. Abolition, therefore, is by no means an inconceivable option. In the Irish context, we might well ask ourselves whether, if the Constitution were being written on a clean slate in 1997 rather than in 1937, the framers would now feel it at all necessary to devise a second legislative chamber.

Simply writing the Seanad out of the Constitution is the most radical 'negative' response to current dissatisfaction regarding the Seanad and its role. Articles 18 and 19 could be deleted, and a series of consequential amendments would need to be made to other Articles. These include Articles that refer to the role of the Seanad as a house of parliament (Article 15), to the legislative process (Articles 20-27), to the possible appointment of senators as government ministers (Article 28) and to the procedure for the removal of the Comptroller and Auditor General (Article 33) and of judges (Article 35). Those Articles that appoint the Cathaoirleach of the Seanad to the Presidential Commission (Article 14) and to the Council of State (Article 31) would also have to be amended.

If the Seanad were to be abolished, of course, the experience of other unitary states tells us that each of its current functions could either be dispensed with or could be transferred elsewhere in the system. We must, however, briefly consider possible destinations for the most important of these functions.

Weak as its current powers are, the Seanad does still have some powers of debate and delay that do act as a check on hasty and/or ill-considered legislation from the Dáil. These powers are particularly significant given the draconian control that the government has over the conduct of business in the Dáil. This control does not in any way derive from the Constitution, which provides that '[the] sole and exclusive power of making laws for the State is hereby vested in the Oireachtas' (Article 15.2.1°). Rather, government control over the legislature derives from the standing orders of each house, which not only give the executive very tight control over the legislative agenda but, crucially in this context, give the executive the power to guillotine legislative debate.

The net result is that, if it is really determined to do so, the government can use its de facto control over legislative business to get laws onto the statute books within a matter of hours, and there are recent examples of this happening.[51] At present, such rough justice can only be meted out to legislative deliberation with the agreement of the Seanad. The question to be

---

[51] This happened in 1985, for example, with the Insurance (Miscellaneous Provisions) Act, involving emergency legislation connected with the financial troubles of the Insurance Corporation of Ireland

answered is whether any of us would want to live in a country in which not only had the upper house been abolished but the government retained the procedural power to force legislation through the lower house if it made up its mind to ignore what would ultimately be the impotent protests of the opposition.

This strongly suggests that, if the Seanad were indeed to be abolished, then there would need to be a significant enhancement of the role of the Dáil as a deliberative chamber. Obvious changes that might help to achieve this would be to increase considerably the time available for Dáil debates, by meeting for longer on more days of the year, and to curtail significantly the government's power to guillotine debate. Legislative procedure could be altered to give a much more central role to committees in the deliberative process, with a view to ensuring that Bills were not enacted without appropriate consideration.

The other useful functions of the current Seanad which we identified in section 3 but did not consider to be 'core' functions of an upper house were to provide members for Oireachtas committees, to provide a potential source of cabinet ministers and thereby to provide a route into the cabinet for the unelected. These are important functions, even if the latter has almost never been used. If the Seanad were to be abolished, then this would create knock-on effects for the committee system that would need to be taken very seriously. In addition, an important decision would have to be taken as to whether it is desirable to have a constitution in which the only possible candidates for positions in government are the 166 members who are elected to the Dáil. While the Seanad's 'back-door' route into cabinet may only rarely have been used, abolishing this might place an undue restriction on the pool of talented people available as potential government ministers in Ireland. Alternative procedures could be found for the removal of those office holders in which the Seanad currently plays a role although, admittedly, this is not an issue that arises frequently. The Cathaoirleach could be replaced by another public figure on the Presidential Commission and on the Council of State.

The argument in favour of abolition is essentially a strong version of the critique set out above in section 3. This is that the core function of a second chamber, as part of the system of checks and balances in the process of legislation, is not being fulfilled at present by Seanad Éireann, given its very weak powers and its partisan control by the government. The assumption is that it is at best costly and at worst dangerous to clutter the Constitution with institutions that do not fulfil a useful role. In the words of Bagehot (1963: 134) 'whatever is unnecessary in Government is pernicious. Human life makes so much complexity necessary that an artificial addition is sure to do harm; you cannot tell when the needless bit of machinery will catch and clog the hundred needful wheels; but the chances are conclusive that it will impede them somewhere ...'. Abolishing the Seanad, furthermore, would also bring Ireland into line with most other states and would be compatible with the global trend away from bicameralism. By vesting legislative power solely in the Dáil, it would be an unambiguous endorsement of the democratic principle; it would provide a more transparent law making procedure, free of the kind of pressures from vested interests with which the

Seanad is sometimes said to be associated. It would save money – not only senators' salaries and expenses, but also those of their associated support staff; and, perhaps more to the point, it would contribute to a saving of space in a parliament that values its central location.

The argument against abolishing the Seanad is essentially that it does not now do nothing, and that what it currently does contributes in a useful way to democratic politics in Ireland. This is particularly important given the very firm government control of the business of the lower house, a degree of control that is not necessarily typical of that found in many unitary states. Some of the anticipated savings, furthermore, might be illusory. The budget of the Seanad is relatively small, as is its permanent staff – during 1995, for instance, it amounted to 9.5% of the total budget for the houses of the Oireachtas, or £2,800,000.[52] Much of the work that senators do at present would simply be transferred to other shoulders, producing a reallocation but not a saving of resources. What is more, much of the work that senators currently do on a largely voluntary basis would be sacrificed. Among the more obvious of the pressures that would develop were the Seanad to be abolished would be the servicing of joint Oireachtas committees, whose role has been increasing in recent years but which, as we have already pointed out, would have much greater difficulty in functioning were they unable to draw on the membership of a second chamber. In addition, an important forum for the formal representation of the interests of particular groups would be lost.

Finally, in considering the issue of abolition, it is very important to point out that we should not just compare the Dáil and Seanad as they now are with the possibility of a unicameral legislature. To do so would be to ignore the range of interesting opportunities that might arise if the current Seanad were to be reformed in any of a number of possible ways. It is to these possibilities that we now turn.

4.3 Reforming the composition of the Seanad

In principle, we can imagine three broad scenarios for the composition of a future Seanad: retention of the present chamber without change; reform of its composition within the existing Constitution (i.e. by means of legislation only); and reform of its composition by constitutional change which, of course, raises a very considerable number of possibilities. In the last case, if the composition of the Seanad is being altered by constitutional change, we

---

[52] Government of Ireland, 1996. This figure includes senators' salaries, secretarial allowances, travel expenses and other allowances; of course, the real cost of the second chamber is slightly larger, since this figure does not include the small permanent staff of the Seanad (with four officers). However, the Seanad's proportion of total Oireachtas expenditure has been declining over time, as the following figures from selected years will illustrate (calculated from *Estimates for public services* in respect of the years in question): 1924-25 (21.6%); 1930-31 (20.5%); 1940-41 (19.3%); 1950-51 (16.9%); 1960-61 (17.5%); 1970-71 (13.7%), 1980 (9.4%), 1990 (8.0%)

can envisage two types of option: modest change that remains close to the format of the existing Seanad, and more far-reaching change leading to the creation of any entirely new type of body.

4.3.1 Retaining the status quo

The most painless option is, of course, simply to retain the existing system but to try to improve its performance and image. The Taoiseach could announce, for example, that in future specific criteria would be followed in the appointment of his eleven nominees. For example, specific quotas might be reserved for such groups as women, emigrants, people from Northern Ireland, socially disadvantaged groups or other minorities. Inter-party agreement might result in similar arrangements for those nominated as candidates in the panel elections.

In practice, it is difficult to imagine how different the Seanad could look unless change is brought about by serious and formal amendment of existing procedures. The good intentions of a Taoiseach or parliamentary party might be all very well in theory, but much more difficult to implement in practice. Any Taoiseach, and even ordinary members of parliamentary parties, will always be under understandable pressure to return favours to colleagues and, in particular, to political allies. A Seanad nomination is an obvious response to this pressure; given the politicised nature of life in the Oireachtas, the pressures of party loyalty are likely to prove irresistible. Other things being equal, it is 'rational' for any politician to wish to maximise his or her party's position in the upper house. Even if these pressures could be set aside at one point in time, it is likely that an inexorable political logic would reassert itself very quickly, and that the Seanad would continue to have more or less the same appearance as at present.

It can be argued in favour of the present position that it has served the country effectively. While many senators may well be either aspiring Dáil candidates or retirees from the lower house, this is not of itself a disqualification from doing excellent work as a senator. Indeed, the present composition of the house may be a positive feature in ensuring that the character of debate is different from that of the Dáil, contributing in this way to the improvement of legislation. Vocational organisations and other public-spirited bodies may take the view that they can enjoy a special voice in the Seanad, through panel representation or as Taoiseach's nominees.

As against this, retention of existing arrangements will leave us with the range of criticisms that have been directed against the composition of the Seanad. Most of these derive from the failure of the Seanad to be seen as reflecting the vocational groups specified in the Constitution, and as being merely a pale reflection of the Dáil. As the Constitution Review Group put it:

> A fundamental justification for the existence of a second house is that it differs from the main house in its representative character. ... As things stand, the candidature produced by the panel nomination procedure and by the nature of the electorate results not in a vocational Seanad, as originally envisaged, but in one not markedly different from Dáil

Éireann. ... The Seanad thus fails to satisfy the fundamental criterion specified above (Constitution Review Group, 1996a: 68-69).

4.3.2 Reform without constitutional amendment

An alternative to the present system that nonetheless does not require constitutional amendment would be to amend the legislative basis of the composition of the Seanad. In fact, the Constitution is much less specific on this matter than is often taken for granted. The broad vocational categories to which the 49 elected senators must belong are specified, but the electoral system is not. As we have already noted, furthermore, Article 19 makes explicit provision for the legislative enfranchisement of additional functional and vocational groups. The provision of Article 18.5 that the election be held by secret postal ballot clearly implies that direct election by the people is not contemplated; but the existing system by which 6 representatives of universities are elected on a very general franchise while the remaining 43 are elected on a very restricted one could be altered or even reversed.[53] In fact, there is nothing in the Constitution to prevent the 6 university senators being elected in the same manner as the panel senators, or, alternatively, being elected by, say, the university governing bodies. The present system by which nominations come from two sources (nominating bodies and members of the Oireachtas) and electors come only from the political domain could be altered by law. Politicians could be cut out of the nomination process, or the electoral process, or both; or nominating bodies could similarly be excluded from both of these processes, leaving nomination and election to the politicians. We may consider the following scenarios.

- *Movement towards vocationalism*: all 49 members are elected by members of nominating bodies (however members are defined) from lists of candidates drawn up by these bodies themselves. Alternatively, this procedure could be applied to the 43 panel members only, the university graduates to continue electing 6 senators.

- *Movement away from vocationalism*: the 43 panel members are elected by the same electoral college as at present, but nominations come from members of the Oireachtas only, i.e the nominating bodies lose their functions.

- *Creating a balance between political election and vocationalism*: the recommendations of the 1959 Seanad Electoral Law Commission, or a variant of these, could be implemented. This would entail division of each of the five panels into two more sharply differentiated subpanels. One of these would consist of candidates nominated by members of the Oireachtas, the electorate to be constituted as at present. The other would consist of candidates proposed by

---

[53] In 1993 81,240 graduates of the National University of Ireland and 22,549 graduates of Dublin University were elegible to vote in the Seanad election; the respective turnout rates were 42.9% and 50.9% (Seanad Éireann, 1993: 8)

nominating bodies, the electorate to consist of representatives of these bodies themselves.[54]

The second and third of these approaches could be associated with ending the election of six members by university graduates, and replacing this system by election from a smaller group, such as members of the university, however this may be defined.

Reform along the lines of the first scenario above would respond to many demands, made over a long time span, for the real composition of the Seanad to match up to the theory. The third scenario might be a useful step towards this. Such an arrangement would also undermine the criticism that the Seanad is little more than a pale reflection of the Dáil.

On the other hand, direct vocational election of senators might bring unanticipated problems. It might not only fail to undermine the party political nature of the Seanad but actually open up the nominating bodies themselves to a more explicit form of party politics. It is unlikely that political parties would just stand by and let nominating bodies proceed with the business of proposing and voting on candidates for a chamber whose role is in large measure political. More fundamentally, reforms of this kind represent little more than tinkering with a system whose whole basis, arguably, is flawed. It would be unable to tackle those issues on which it is constrained by the Constitution: the very notion of vocational representation, which, according to critics, fails to correspond to any reality in Irish life, either at present or in the past, and which is now eccentric and dated as a basis for political representation. This approach would also be unable to address the very unusual provision by which the Taoiseach can nominate senators.

4.3.3 Minor constitutional change

The Constitution could be amended to allow for the generation of an upper house on a different basis, but one that would stop short of direct election. If the Constitution were to be changed, then not only the selection principle but also the term of office of senators and the overall size of the Seanad could be altered. For purposes of discussion, we will assume that the Seanad retains its present size, which as we have seen is not out of line with comparable chambers elsewhere. As far as the selection principle is concerned, we can imagine the following scenarios.

- *Modification of the status quo*: this would follow the lines discussed in 4.3.2, but would write this change into the Constitution rather than leaving it to legislation. The Constitution could also be amended to restrict the Taoiseach to certain categories in making appointments,

---

[54] The Commission suggested that 20 seats be reserved for Oireachtas nominees and 23 for those from nominating bodies, but the latter could be increased (to approach the position in the first possibility above) or reduced (to approach the second possibility)

or it could transfer this right from the Taoiseach to the President (but possibly requiring the President first to consult with the Taoiseach).

- *Nomination*: members of the Seanad could be nominated by the President, possibly after consultation with various interests (such as the Taoiseach, the leader of the opposition and certain designated bodies such as the nominating bodies as they exist at present). This could also be used to extend appointments to representatives of emigrants, of the Northern Irish population and/or of various marginal groups.

- *Indirect election*: the Seanad could be indirectly elected to represent, say, the provinces, but provision could be made to ensure that persons nominated had special qualities to bring to the Seanad (for example, bodies similar to the existing nominating bodies could be involved in the process). The electoral colleges could consist of local councillors and members of the Oireachtas.

- *Composite system*: the Seanad could be partly nominated by the President (say, 10, 15 or 20 members) and partly indirectly elected, in both cases along lines similar to those discussed above.

A further matter concerns the term of office of senators. The term of the Seanad could either be linked to that of the Dáil as at present, or senators could be appointed for a fixed term. To give an example, if in a composite system 10 senators were to be appointed and 50 elected indirectly, the term of office of senators could be fixed at six years, with a requirement that half retire every three years. The normal Seanad renewal process would thus consist of the nomination of 5 senators and the indirect election of 25.

Minor amendments to the Constitution could seriously tackle certain significant defects in the present system of Seanad election. Altering the system of nomination could bring the Constitution into line with the more conventional appointment systems adopted elsewhere, and it could be used to provide for the return of spokespersons for various groups that have not up to now had much say in the legislative process. Provision for an indirectly elected component could allow greater flexibility for the representation of particular groups in the second chamber.

On the other hand, powerful arguments can be put against change along these lines. Some arguments would run along precisely the lines indicated in section 4.3.2. Extending the right of indirect election to voluntary bodies might push these bodies to adopt stances close to those of the major parties, and might promote inter-party rivalries within their governing authorities. The net effect might be to politicise the voluntary sector rather than to vocationalise the Seanad. On the other hand, if this did not happen and the Seanad were to become a chamber representing various non-partisan interests, then it is possible that the perspectives of individual senators would actually be narrower than at present, and the Dáil might be tempted to take their position even less seriously than it does now. The cost of establishing a non-partisan Seanad, in other words, might be the creation of a powerless Seanad. Worse, if the Seanad were indirectly elected from four regions with county councillors as the predominant part of the electorate, the electoral quota would be small and possibilities of corruption correspondingly high. This could be the case a fortiori if a small number of nominating bodies were to be responsible for the election.

4.3.4 Major constitutional change: direct election

The most radical 'positive' response to current dissatisfaction regarding the Seanad would be to amend the Constitution to have it elected directly. This could be linked with a more restrictive set of conditions for eligibility, and even the right to vote, so as to help distinguish the upper house from the lower. It could also involve a Seanad whose life span is tied to that of the Dáil, or one with a fixed life span, with or without partial renewal. It is also possible to conceive of direct elections on the basis of functional and/or vocational constituencies, rather than the geographic constituencies with which we are more familiar. Again, we can envisage a number of scenarios.

- *Direct election to represent territories*: each administrative county might elect two members, regardless of its size. Alternatively, the four European parliament constituencies could elect, say, 15 each, possibly for a fixed term of six years, one-half retiring every three years.

- *Direct election to represent the population*: the provinces could be used, elections to take place at the same time as elections to the European Parliament (the allocation of seats might be 18 to Dublin, 14 to the rest of Leinster, 17 to Munster and 11 to Connacht-Ulster). Alternatively, the term of senators might be extended to, say, six years, with arrangements for partial renewal of half the senate every three years.

- *Composite system*: provision could be made for direct election of most senators, but others could be appointed to give the government of the day an overall majority. For instance, 48 senators might be elected (say, 12 from each of the four European parliament constituencies, or this figure could be related to population) for either a fixed term, with or without partial renewal or for a term coinciding with that of the Dáil. The balance of 12 senators could be appointed by the President on the advice of the Taoiseach (or, if the former were to be given more discretion, by the President following consultation with the Taoiseach).

- *Functional and/or vocational constituencies:* provision could be made for direct popular election to functional and/or vocational panels. Voters could register to vote as a member of one (but only one) of these panels, with the number of senators from each panel being in proportion to its number of registered voters. These panels could be defined in the Constitution, as at present, or there could be a system whereby any group could put a panel before the electorate if it could gather a specified number (eg 50,000) of signatures of registered voters.

A directly elected Seanad would certainly have more popular legitimacy, and hence authority, than the Seanad as constituted at present. It would be in a strong moral position to assert itself on matters related to legislation and the process of government in general. Depending on the precise system of representation selected, it would also give the opportunity to offer a legitimate voice in the political system to social groups and regional interests which are not currently represented in any explicit way by the system of narrow geographic constituencies used for the Dáil. The greater authority that would result could ensure that the work of the Oireachtas was carried out more legitimately and effectively.

Against this it might be argued that regional consciousness in Ireland is very weak, while it is not desirable to transform functional and/or vocational groups into partisan political arenas. The second chamber would certainly be highly political even if not partisan, and the smaller number of senators would undoubtedly be conscious that their electoral quotas were higher than those of their more numerous Dáil counterparts. Especially if Seanad elections did not coincide with those to the Dáil, the potential for clashes between the two houses would be great. On the other hand, if a significant proportion of the Seanad were to be nominated to ensure that the government had a majority, then the whole point of having direct election as the primary way to select senators, which is to have a distinctive second house, would be undermined.

4.4 Reforming the powers of the Seanad

We can imagine a number of broad scenarios for the future powers of the Seanad. First, there might be no change in the Seanad's present powers. Second, there might be change within the existing constitutional parameters, for example through legislation or amendments to standing orders. Finally there might be an extension of the Seanad's powers by constitutional change. Constitutional change, furthermore, might increase the role of the Seanad in the legislative process in a way that left it with less power than the Dáil; or it might do so in a way that gave it equal status with the Dáil, not only in terms of legislation but in terms of the making and breaking of governments. We develop these various options in what follows.

4.4.1 Retaining the status quo

Those cynical about the prospects for institutional reform in Ireland might take the view that the most probable outcome of the current debate will be no change: that the Seanad will retain both its present composition and its powers. However, since a considerable part of the critique of the current Seanad is that its composition is not distinct enough from that of the Dáil, we first consider the possibility that, while retaining its current powers, the composition of the Seanad is reformed to make it more distinct from that of the Dáil. Actually, we do not need to know *precisely* how the composition of the Seanad might be reformed in order to give at least some consideration to what might happen in this event. Since we argue that the purpose of having any institution is to make a difference and that the core role of a senate is as part of the checks and balances on the process of legislation, this implies that a Seanad with a reformed composition would, indeed should, from time to time disagree with the Dáil. If it never disagreed, it is hard to see how it would make a difference.

How would the role of the Seanad change in this event? It would still have at most a 90-day power of delay over legislation, and all Seanad amendments could still be rejected by the Dáil. Provided the composition of the Seanad gave it more popular legitimacy than at present, however, it would become more difficult for the government to ignore the views of a Seanad that disagreed with it. Thus there might be a change in the power relationship between government and Seanad at the level of practical politics, even if not at the level of formal powers.

Perhaps much more significantly, however, Article 27 could assume much more importance if there was a majority in the Seanad that did not have the same composition as the majority in the Dáil. Differing Dáil and Seanad majorities would raise the real possibility of Article 27 petitions to the President. This would have two potential implications, both of which would involve a more significant political role for the Seanad.

The first is that the President would be forced to make what would be quite a significant political decision about whether or not a provision in a Bill is of 'such national importance' that it should be referred to the people by way of referendum or general election. Since there is no precedent for an Article 27 petition, we have no real sense of quite how important 'such' national importance might actually be. Making this decision would result in some politicisation of the office of President. However, decisions under Article 27 would not necessarily be any more controversial than the current power of the President under Article 26, which has indeed been used in politically controversial circumstances, to refer Bills to the Supreme Court. Such politicisation could of course be avoided by amending Article 27 to remove presidential discretion in this matter.

It is safe to assume, however, given the conventions that have emerged in Ireland about the apolitical role of the President, that the inclination of a President would be to accede to such a petition unless there were self-evident reasons not to do so. Thus the second implication of a revitalised Article 27 is that it might not be too difficult for a Seanad majority to combine with the Dáil opposition to force a referendum or a general election on an important issue. This illustrates the point that even the Seanad's current formal powers might well become quite a bit more significant if its composition were to change.

Thus the arguments in favour of retaining the current powers depend upon a change in the composition of the current Seanad, but a change that would not cause it to mirror the Dáil in terms of its political complexion. If it were changed along such lines, then the Seanad would play a practical as opposed to a purely theoretical role in the system of checks and balances. Depending upon how the composition of the Seanad was changed, new voices could have a say in the national parliament, and the legitimacy of the Oireachtas could be thereby enhanced.

The main counter-argument is one that will run through this entire section, which is the potential for conflict between the two houses. Any enhancement of the role of the Seanad while leaving the role of the Dáil unchanged will affect the relative position of the two houses. This will make conflicts between the houses more serious, and increase the possibility of stalemate. In the context of the present scenario, furthermore, the legitimacy of the Oireachtas might even be compromised in certain circumstances: if, for instance the Seanad were to be directly elected at a time that did not coincide with the election to the Dáil, new groups could acquire a position of dominance there, but despite the authority gained from more recent election they might be overruled by the Dáil when the chips were really down.

4.4.2 Giving the Seanad new non-overlapping powers

When people complain about the Irish political system, they often have in mind a lack of political accountability in some area or another. Decisions are made that are firmly in the public domain, but there appears to be nobody who is politically answerable for these. Appointments are made to positions of obvious public responsibility, but there appears to be no public scrutiny over the process of appointment. Tribunals of enquiry into politically explosive matters are conducted at vast expense, typically presided over by senior members of the judiciary who in theory should be protected at all costs from any hint of a politicisation of their position. In short there are important jobs for the political system that are not currently being done by it. Given the protestations of TDs that they are already massively overworked, one clear possibility is to give these jobs to the Seanad or, more realistically, to Seanad committees.

Since the adoption of the 1937 Constitution, there has been a huge burgeoning of that part of the public sector that exists outside the core civil service – with an ever-increasing number of state boards, semi-state bodies, and so on. Nominations to most of these are in the gift of a minister, and are typically made with very little explanation or justification to the public. Another trend has been an increasing reluctance of ministers to accept full political responsibility and resign on foot of serious problems in the core civil service for which they are formally responsible, much less in some state board to which they have made nominations. Those nominated to state boards, furthermore, typically stay in office beyond the tenure of the minister who made the nomination, so that a minister from quite a different party may well be in office when problems eventually arise. In this case any direct political accountability lapses with the change of minister. Yet many would feel that senior people in the public sector, even if they are not members of the core civil service, should be seen publicly to be suitable candidates when they are appointed, and should subsequently be held publicly accountable for their actions.

It is not too difficult to imagine a Seanad Committee on Senior Public Appointments, for example, to which ministers would submit for approval all nominations for designated senior appointments in their areas of departmental jurisdiction. Such a committee might also have the power to review such appointments in certain specified circumstances. There would be no need for US-style high profile public hearings on such appointments, but it is certainly arguable that some public body other than the appointing minister should review the curriculum vitae of each nominee to a senior public position, to ensure that such persons are suitable for the job, and from time to time review their performance in office.

An alternative, of course, would be to formalise and extend the doctrine of individual ministerial responsibility for such appointments, making it a much more routine matter for ministers to be forced to resign when a person that they have appointed to some senior public position makes a grave error. Even then, of course, the issue of political responsibility for senior public appointments made by previous ministers remains unclear. At the moment, however, there is an important political job in this area that is not being done, and one body that might be able to do it is the Seanad.

A similar approach might be taken to tribunals of enquiry, the functions of which could be conducted by ad hoc Seanad committees. Obviously, high-level legal expertise would often have to be available to such an enquiry – but this could be provided on a consultancy basis, leaving full political responsibility for the conduct of the enquiry with the upper house, and in this way not forcing members of the senior judiciary into a politically controversial role.

The key argument in favour of this scenario is that it addresses widespread popular unease about the lack of accountability in many areas of public life. Such new powers for the Seanad are not touched upon at all in the Constitution, and would not explicitly overlap with those of the Dáil, since they relate to forms of public accountability that are currently not being provided at all by the Oireachtas, the body over which the public has some direct control. In short, such reforms to the Seanad would respond to popular demand, would cater for a need that is not currently being met, but would not bring the Seanad into direct conflict with the Dáil.

The counter-argument is that it would be naive to assume that such increased powers would not bring the Seanad into conflict with the government, and thereby indirectly with the Dáil. Unless the composition of the Seanad were always to be dominated by the government, we can presume that it would sometimes disagree with nominations for government appointments, and would sometimes conduct enquiries that were critical of the government. It is also sometimes argued that talented people might be less inclined to offer themselves for public service if they were obliged to subject themselves to a higher level of public scrutiny.

4.4.3 Constitutional change to increase the powers of the Seanad vis à vis the Dáil

Another way to give a more prominent role to the Seanad is to enhance its constitutional position in the legislative process. As we have already noted, giving the Seanad significant power over money Bills would be likely to bring it into direct confrontation with the government, despite the fact that the Seanad would in this scenario have no constitutional role in the making and breaking of governments. As can been seen from the US experience, this involves a very clear potential for budgetary deadlock. There is much less of an objection in theory, however, to enhancing the role of the Seanad in relation to non-money Bills. This could be achieved in a number of ways. The simplest would be to extend the time period for which the Seanad could delay legislation, say to 180 days or one year, leaving all other provisions unchanged. This would also increase the de facto political power of the Seanad, since the sanction at its disposal would then be more painful for the Dáil in the event of a disagreement between the two houses. This might in turn lead to increased attention being paid to the views of the Seanad.

An alternative way to increase the power of the Seanad vis à vis the Dáil would be to introduce some mechanism to prevent amendments that are validly passed by the upper house from being simply ignored by the lower. Obviously, if the Seanad were to pass an amendment and the Dáil were not to accept this, then some way would need to be found to resolve the situation. Simply allowing the Seanad amendment to prevail in such circumstances would in effect put the Seanad above the Dáil in the legislative process, allowing it if it wished to confound anything that the Dáil might do. But there are other ways to proceed.

The superior position of the Dáil could be reconciled with giving some power over legislation to the Seanad, for example by allowing to prevail those Seanad amendments that had passed by some qualified majority – such as two-thirds or three-quarters of those voting – while Dáil amendments would continue to require only a simple majority. Alternatively, a requirement might be introduced that no Bill coming from the Dáil could become law without receiving the support of at least one-third (or one-quarter) of the Seanad, in effect giving a qualified majority of the Seanad a veto over legislation.

The argument in favour of this option would be that constitutionally entrenching the Seanad in a more serious way into the system of legislative checks and balances would not only have significant symbolic importance, but it would also provide a more effective constitutional bulwark against extreme and ill-considered action by the Dáil. Especially if the composition of the Seanad continues to be constructed along the lines of the party system in the Dáil, it should also be noted that the circumstances in which such qualified majorities could realistically be invoked would be very rare. A fortiori, if they were invoked, then this would be a signal that something very serious needed to be taken into account.

The counter-argument, once more, is the possibility of deadlock between the two houses. Once even a qualified majority of the Seanad has a de facto veto over legislation, then the possibility arises that much-needed legislation could not be passed as a result of political conflict between the Dáil and Seanad. It is unlikely that both houses would have identical popular legitimacy with respect to any given deadlocked measure, which would result in one house or the other being seen to stand in the way of legitimate legislative progress.

4.4.4 Giving Seanad and Dáil an equal role in the legislative and governmental process

The next step along the road mapped out in the preceding paragraphs would be to give the Seanad and the Dáil an equal role in the legislative and/or governmental process. We consider legislation first.

The equal role of the Seanad in passing non-money Bills could be achieved very simply by requiring the passage of a Bill by both houses before it could become law. A Bill that failed to pass both houses could not become law. For absolute equality between the houses, each house would also need to have an equal right to initiate legislation. The balance could be tilted somewhat towards the Dáil by requiring the passage of Bills by both houses, but by reserving to the Dáil the right to initiate these.

The justification for creating a constitutional arrangement such as this would depend upon a reformed composition for the Seanad and would assume that the representative basis of the Seanad was at least as legitimate as that of the Dáil. If the composition of the Seanad were to be reformed so as to achieve this, there is no reason in principle why the upper house should not have the same role in the legislative process as the lower. In such circumstances, indeed, even legislative gridlock might be justified on the grounds that the representative system was telling us that there is no unambiguous majority among the public as a whole in favour of the action at issue. We would in effect have a system of checks and balances that was not just a pious constitutional aspiration, but one that was actually working.

The counter-argument is that this is the scenario offering the most serious probability of real legislative gridlock, a possibility that will always be there if two houses are given anything like equal power over the passage of legislation. There might in these circumstances be issues that urgently required legislation, but which were such that it was just not possible to find a majority for the same Bill in both Dáil and Seanad. In such circumstances, deadlock between the houses of the Oireachtas could be very damaging for the country.

The last of the powers currently reserved to the Dáil that might be shared by the Seanad is almost certainly the most important of them all – the power to make and break governments. Ireland has a system of 'parliamentary government', defined by having an executive that is responsible to the legislature, or at least to the lower house. This differs considerably from a presidential system of government where, as in the USA, the chief executive is chosen directly by the people. The manifestation of the system of parliamentary government in Ireland is that the Taoiseach is nominated by the Dáil (Article 13.1.1°), that the cabinet must be approved by the Dáil (Article 13.1.2°), that the Taoiseach must resign on losing the support of the Dáil (Article 28.10), and that, if the Taoiseach resigns, then the other members of the government are also deemed to have resigned (Article 28.11.1°). As in most other parliamentary government systems, there is no role for the Seanad in any of this. As we have already noted, this is a rationale for giving the Seanad less power over money Bills, which go to the heart of the government's ability to govern, than over other legislation.

Once more, there is a range of possibilities, broadly equivalent to those we have discussed when looking at how to enhance the role of the upper house in the consideration of legislation. Thus provision might be made that a nomination for Taoiseach and/or a proposed cabinet could be blocked by a qualified majority of the upper house, which would thus have a qualified veto over the government formation process. Similar provisions could be introduced in respect of votes of no confidence used to dismiss. Full co-equal status with the Dáil would be achieved by requiring that any nomination for Taoiseach, or proposed cabinet, receive the assent of a majority of both houses.

In favour of this scenario it might be argued that there is no reason, in principle, why a representative upper house should not be involved in the making and breaking of governments. If the Seanad is representative, why should it be excluded from the government formation process? If it is not representative, why should it exist? Even if the Seanad were not given full co-equal status with the Dáil in the government formation process, the possibility of giving the Seanad a lesser role by giving the upper house the capacity to withhold approval of the nomination of a new government and/or the dismissal of the incumbent by qualified majority is an intriguing possibility.

Set against this, however, is the real likelihood of deadlock over government formation or dismissal. The practical effect of such a deadlock would be to leave a 'lame duck' caretaker administration running the country with no possibility of resolving the conflict. This is a most unappealing prospect, and provides a very powerful argument indeed against giving the Seanad a equal role to that of the Dáil in the making and breaking of governments.

4.5   Possible combinations of composition and powers for the Seanad

As we have already argued at several points, the future role of Seanad Éireann will be determined by the way in which its composition interacts with its powers. We can extract a number of broad political possibilities from the range of institutional options that we have discussed above.

One obvious option is abolition, the arguments for and against which were reviewed in section 4.2 above. If the Seanad were to be abolished, then its existing functions, as we have seen, would need to be redistributed. Obviously, if abolished, the issue of extending its powers does not arise.

Turning to scenarios for reforming the composition of the Seanad, the broad possibilities were outlined above. Since the substantive effects of minor changes (with or without constitutional change) may be similar, we group two of the categories discussed above (reform without constitutional amendment; minor constitutional change). There are then three possibilities:

- retain the status quo
- change its composition by providing for an amended form of nomination or indirect election, which might be achieved within existing legislation or might require 'minor' constitutional reform

- amend the Constitution to allow a radical change in the composition of the Seanad, conferring on it the increased popular legitimacy arising from direct election.

Scenarios for reforming the powers of the Seanad may be similarly reclassified from those considered above, and may be made more specific. We then get the following possibilities:

- retain the status quo

- give it new powers that do not overlap with those of the Dáil

- enhance its power over the legislative process

- enhance its power over the making and breaking of governments.

Table 9 summarises the main interactions between the various possible reforms of the composition and powers of the Seanad. In this table, the three columns refer to the composition of the Seanad, and the four rows to its powers. The cells refer to the kinds of combination of composition and powers that logically may exist. We comment on each of these in turn.

A1 Obviously, if the status quo is retained with regard to both the powers and composition of the upper house, then the current Seanad continues in operation, and the arguments for it and against it continue to apply.

A2 If the Seanad were to retain its current composition and position in the legislative process, but were in addition to be given new powers that do not overlap with those of the Dáil, then the result would be that the Oireachtas would fulfil functions that are not currently being attended to.

A3 Enhancing the legislative role of the Seanad vis-à-vis the Dáil, but retaining its current composition, would only make a real difference in those very rare cases when the government changed without an intervening election, as in 1994. Only then does the possibility of conflict between the Seanad and the government become a serious prospect, but then the conflict would be between a 'new' government and an 'old' Seanad.

A4 However, if a Seanad with its current composition were given power over the making and breaking of governments, the provision for the Taoiseach's eleven nominees in the Seanad, and consequent secure government majority in the upper house, could only entrench the incumbent government and make it far more difficult to dismiss.

Table 9: Options for the composition and powers of Seanad Éireann

Powers	Composition:		
	A Status quo	*B* Amended form of nomination or indirect election	*C* Direct election
1 Status quo	*A1* Status quo.	*B1* New groups gain a voice in the political system. Existing delay and Article 27 powers more likely to be used.	*C1* New groups may gain a voice in the political system. Existing delay and Article 27 powers more likely to be used. Rival legitimacies cause de facto though not de jure weakening of the ability of Dáil to prevail over Seanad.
2 New non-overlapping powers	*A2* Oireachtas does potentially valuable jobs that it is not currently doing.	*B2* New groups gain a voice in the political system. Existing delay and Article 27 powers more likely to be used. Oireachtas does potentially valuable jobs that it is not currently doing.	*C2* New groups may gain a voice in the political system. Existing delay and Article 27 powers more likely to be used. Rival legitimacies cause de facto though not de jure weakening of the ability of Dáil to prevail over Seanad. Oireachtas does potentially valuable jobs that it is not currently doing.
3 Increased power over legislation	*A3* Enhanced formal legislative role for Seanad only effective in practice when new government forms without intervening election.	*B3* Empowerment of new groups in the system of checks and balances.	*C3* Empowerment of new groups in the system of checks and balances. Rival legitimacies weaken the ability of Dáil to prevail over Seanad.
4 Increased power over executive	*A4* Government formation cannot take place until after Seanad election, though little de facto effect on this. Government position more secure if Seanad vote necessary for government defeat.	*B4* Potential for deadlock over government formation and/or defeat, unless one house clearly dominant.	*C4* Potential for deadlock over government formation that could be difficult to resolve, given rival legitimacies.

B1 Changing the composition of the Seanad while retaining its existing powers offers the prospect of increasing the political significance of these current powers. This might happen if the Seanad more frequently disagrees with the Dáil, even if it can still ultimately be over-ridden, and use could be made of Article 27 (to petition for a referendum).

B2 If, in addition, the composition of the Seanad were to be changed, then this would create newly empowered groups that are represented in the Seanad, and who have a new role in the political process that does not bring them into direct conflict with the Dáil. In addition, however, the effects outlined in the preceding paragraphs could also come into play.

B3 If the legislative powers of the Seanad were to be increased vis-à-vis the Dáil at the same time as its composition were changed, then not only would new voices be heard in the Oireachtas but the different groups empowered in the Dáil and the Seanad might come into conflict with each other during the process of legislation.

B4 If the Seanad were to be given a real role in the making and breaking of governments, and if the Seanad and Dáil have different compositions, then there is a clear potential for deadlock in the government formation process unless one house was designated as being clearly dominant in such circumstances.

C1 If the composition of the Seanad were changed by constitutional reform to allow for direct election, furthermore, its enhanced legitimacy would make it far harder and more dangerous, politically, for the Dáil to override the Seanad, whatever about the formal constitutional position. This would increase the de facto power of the Seanad as well as the de facto possibility of conflict, although not formal deadlock, between the houses.

C2 All of the considerations in *C1* would continue to apply if the Seanad were to be given additional powers that did not overlap with those of the Dáil. However, the Seanad would now be performing a significantly more valuable institutional role.

C3 These considerations would continue to apply if the Seanad were given a specific role in the legislative process. However, the prospect for more serious conflicts between the Dáil and the Seanad would be greatly increased, and some mechanism would need to be devised for resolving such disputes.

C4 If the representative basis of the Seanad were to be as legitimate as that of the Dáil, as it might well be if a system of direct election were to be introduced, there would be no way of saying that one was right and the other wrong. While there would be a potential for deadlock, this might represent real disagreements in society that ought to be reflected in the legislative system.

We may now proceed in the final section of this paper to explore in rather more detail what we consider to be the main options for consideration in any thoroughgoing review of the future of Seanad Éireann. These options are those shaded in table 9, and are selected for reasons that we explain in the next section.

5 BLUEPRINTS FOR THE FUTURE

In order to expedite our conclusions, we have ruled out certain of the options identified in table 9 as ones that we will not take any further, for relatively self-evident reasons. This allows us to focus on possibilities that do on the face of things appear to be both viable and to have some merit.

Thus we do not consider any further those options that would give the Seanad a role in the making and breaking of governments. If the composition of the upper house were to be changed so that its partisan balance differed in important ways from that of the lower house, then giving both houses an interlocking role in the business of government formation and dismissal would be an obvious recipe for deadlock. The possibility of 'lame duck' governments that could not be replaced effectively rules out these options, which are anyway almost never found among upper houses in other countries.

We also rule out options in table 9 that involve major constitutional reform to alter the composition of the Seanad, while at the same time giving the Seanad either no more powers than at present, or giving it new non-overlapping powers with the Dáil. The reason for ruling these out is that it seems to us to be inconsistent to reform the Constitution to allow for a directly elected Seanad, the popular legitimacy of which would presumably be as great as that of the Dáil, while still allowing the Dáil absolute power to overrule the Seanad on all matters of legislation. Indeed, it could well be a recipe for popular disenchantment with the Oireachtas and the political system as a whole if a new Seanad, just put in place by the people in a national election, could simply be overridden by the Dáil.

Finally, we take no further the option that the Seanad retains its current composition, but is given increased powers vis-à-vis the Dáil in the legislative process. The reason for this is that, for governments forming after Dáil elections, government control over the Dáil already extends to even stronger government control over the Seanad by virtue of the Taoiseach's eleven nominees. In such circumstances, it makes no difference to give the Seanad extra powers over legislation. In contrast, if the partisan composition of the government should change between elections as happened for the first time in 1994, then any enhanced role played by the Seanad in the legislative process would take the form of the *previous* Taoiseach's eleven nominees constraining the legislative programme of the *current* government. There seems to us to be no good reason to argue for this.

Thus, the options that we leave on the agenda are as follows: abolition; the status quo (which, whatever anyone thinks about it, is of course always on the agenda); keeping the Seanad's current powers, but introducing 'minor' modifications to its composition; giving the Seanad new non-overlapping power, with or without 'minor' changes to its composition; and giving the Seanad an increased role in the legislative process, assuming either 'minor' or 'major' changes in its composition. These are discussed below, in ascending order of the role to be played by a future Seanad Éireann.

Before coming to conclusions about these options, we should restate the fundamental dilemma associated with having a second chamber at all, a dilemma that we outlined in section 3. It is only worth having a second chamber if it can make a difference. If it *can* make a difference, it *will* make a difference from time to time. Almost by definition, this is bound to put it in conflict with other parts of the political system. Those who argue that the Seanad should never, ever, come into conflict with any other part of the political system are almost arguing that there should not be a second chamber.

5.1 Abolition

Those who argue that the Seanad should never come into conflict with either the Dáil or the government, as we have just seen, come close to arguing that Seanad Éireann should be abolished. This is clearly a tenable position, and countries such as New Zealand, Sweden or Denmark that have indeed abolished their upper houses in recent times do not seem in any obvious way the worse for the experience. We reviewed the arguments for and against abolition in section 4.2.

The main argument in favour of abolition is that there is simply no point in having an upper house with a composition that mirrors that of the lower house and a role in the legislative process that places it in complete subservience to both the lower house and the government. Those functions that the Seanad does perform, so this argument goes, can easily be transferred to other parts of the political system.

The main argument against abolition is that the legislative process in Ireland, and in particular the business of the Dáil, is procedurally too much under the control of the government. The Seanad provides some, albeit very limited, pause for reflection that would be sorely missed if it were to be abolished altogether. It also provides legislators to staff joint committees, as well as constituting a mechanism for non-partisan voices to be heard in the legislature, especially if the Taoiseach decides to avail of this opportunity when making nominations.

We feel that the case for abolition must obviously be taken seriously, but that this should only be considered in the context of simultaneous reforms of Dáil procedures that significantly increase the Dáil's capacity to deliberate carefully on new legislation. This is likely to require improvements to the committee system, an extension of Dáil sittings, a relaxation of the guillotine procedure and a general opening up of the business of the Dáil to constructive input from backbenchers, currently Ireland's most under-utilised legislative resource.

5.2 Status quo

The problems with the status quo have been stated many times, most recently by the Constitution Review Group, leading to the conclusion that the Seanad should either be reformed or abolished.

In a way the strongest argument in favour of the status quo is that the Seanad as we know it has done no great harm, and has sometimes done good, either by contributing welcome and valuable amendments to legislation, or by contributing to the political system as a whole by providing some very able and worthy members of the Oireachtas. Senators have not only contributed in important ways to public debate, but they now help to keep the Oireachtas committee system afloat.

The strongest argument against the status quo is the argument in favour of abolition of the Seanad, summarised in section 5.1.

Critics of the Seanad say that notwithstanding the valuable contributions to public debate made by distinguished past senators and the current input into the committee system by the Seanad, the upper house does not currently have a sufficiently important role in the legislative process in Ireland to justify an entire second house of the legislature. This does not, however, amount to an argument for abolition. Rather, it should be seen as an opportunity to do something new. We should not compare the current situation with one in which there was no Seanad. Rather we should compare it with one in which the Seanad has been reformed to enhance its contribution to the Irish political system. It is to these possibilities that we now turn.

5.3 Current powers, reformed composition

The most modest way to reform Seanad Éireann would be to retain its existing powers but to change the way in which Senators are selected. As we saw in section 4.3.2, the way to do this that is most in line with previous suggestions would be to make the practice of vocationalism in Seanad representation match the aspirations that were very clearly set out in the 1937 Constitution. The alternative, moving away from vocationalism in the direction of having the Dáil alone elect the Seanad while leaving the Seanad's powers unchanged, does not in any way address the criticisms that have been levelled at the current upper house.

If, on the other hand, the composition of the Seanad were to be reformed to give effect to vocationalism, a change which might well not require amendment of the Constitution, then new voices could be brought into the political system, and these might well increase the legitimacy and inclusiveness of the system as a whole. The partisan composition of the Seanad would not mirror that of the Dáil, giving the upper house a distinctive position. But the fact that the powers of the Seanad had not been increased would not bring the two houses into conflict with one another. While some of the options discussed below may bring even greater benefits, reforming the composition of the Seanad while retaining its current powers does seem to us to bring a clear improvement over the current situation, despite the fact that, as we have seen, vocational representation is really very rare in the legislative chambers of modern democracies.

5.4 New non-overlapping powers, current composition

The great attraction of giving the Seanad new powers that do not overlap with those of the Dáil is that TDs already claim to be overworked, while at the same time many people feel that there are important jobs for the political system to do that the current political system is not doing well enough. In such circumstances, the obvious response to the problem of a chamber that does not seem to be overworked is to give it some important additional functions.

There is no shortage of work to be done by the political system, especially in the area of public accountability. The suggestions made in section 4.4.2 concerned the review of senior public appointments and the conducting of tribunals of enquiry. These are two very obvious areas in which the political system is currently not doing as much as it might, but there are doubtless many others.

Since the new functions would not overlap with those of the Dáil, the fact that the composition of the Seanad had not changed would not undermine the rationale of moving in this direction. Even if the partisan composition of the Dáil precisely mirrored that of the Seanad, indeed, these new functions could quite possibly be fulfilled very effectively, with no conflict at all between the two houses. For this reason, it seems to us to be very well worthwhile to explore the possibility of giving new non-overlapping powers to the Seanad.

5.5 New non-overlapping powers, reformed composition

This option would combine the benefits of options 5.3 and 5.4, discussed above. New voices would be brought into the political system at the same time as new and much-needed tasks were carried out by the Oireachtas. The new element introduced by doing both things at the same time is that, because the two houses of the Oireachtas would not have the same composition, and because the Dáil would remain the chamber that keeps the government in office, the Seanad's new jobs might sometimes bring it into conflict with the government, and hence also with the Dáil. This might arise if the review of senior public appointments was critical of some particular ministerial nominee for public office, for example, or if a Seanad tribunal of enquiry was critical of the actions of the government.

This option thus marks the point in the hierarchy of reforms at which we first see some potential for real conflict between the two houses of the Oireachtas. It is appropriate to be realistic about this, though we should also remind ourselves that such conflict is always going to be possible once the Seanad is given an important role to perform. The conflict between the two houses in this instance would be political but, given the non-overlapping nature of the new Seanad powers, it would not result in legislative or governmental deadlock. The key decision to be made, therefore, is whether any conflict at all between the two houses can be tolerated. If it can, then this option seems to us to be a very worthwhile possibility for investigation.

5.6 Enhanced legislative role, reformed composition

As we argued in section 4.4.4, enhancing the role of the Seanad in the legislative process could only really be justified politically if the composition of the Seanad were also reformed. This enhanced role would almost certainly fall short of giving both houses an absolutely equal role in the legislative process, given the possibilities for deadlock. It is most likely to come, therefore, either from increasing the Seanad's powers of delay, or from entrenching a veto over legislation for a qualified majority of the Seanad. Either of these changes would require constitutional amendment.

In effect, this change would give some teeth to what is at present the fiction that the role of the upper house is to act as some counterweight to the legislative activities of the lower. It would give real power to the upper house, but at the same time would leave the lower house clearly dominant. Indeed, we can think both of the size of the qualified Seanad majority needed to activate its veto, as well as of the period of delay it might impose, as two continuous 'volume controls' that determine the relative power of Dáil and Seanad.

The present situation is that not even 100 percent of the Seanad can impose a veto, and the delay period is 90 days. For every day that we increase this delay period, we increase the power of the Seanad until, when the delay period is five years, the current legal maximum life of a Dáil, a majority of the Seanad is in effect given a total veto on legislation. In the same way, for a fixed delay period, for every percentage point that we reduce the size of the qualified majority needed to activate a Seanad veto, we increase the power of the Seanad. Thus a requirement that 100 percent of senators are needed to activate a veto would be almost impossible to achieve in practice, and would give very little de facto power to the Seanad. A requirement that 75 percent of senators are needed to activate the veto would mean that the government would have to have the support of at least one-quarter of senators to pass its legislation. A qualified majority requirement of two-thirds of the Seanad would require the government to have the support of one-third of senators, as so on. As the size of the qualified majority was reduced, so the number of senators who would have to support government legislation would increase.

Obviously, these volume controls, by affecting the relative power of Dáil and Seanad, also affect the potential for conflict between them over the passage of legislation, since the relative power of the Seanad and the potential for conflict between the houses are in practice two sides of the same coin. Thus, once more, the key decision to be made is how far the virtues of having an upper house merit the possibility of conflict between the houses. If it is decided that such potential conflict is an acceptable price to pay, and that it may even reflect in an appropriate manner real conflict within the wider social system, then this option is clearly worth exploring.

5.7 Enhanced legislative role, direct election

The most 'radical' option that we consider in any detail is giving the Seanad a real role in the legislative process, at the same time as reforming its composition to make it a directly elected body. The arguments in section 5.6 above apply with equal force to this option. The single, but vital, additional ingredient is the political implication of conflict between the houses, once the Seanad has become a directly elected body with a popular legitimacy equal to that of the Dáil.

The scenario we must envisage when thinking about this option is one in which the two houses are directly elected, each on a different basis, and have different majorities with respect to an important piece of legislation. Assuming that the Seanad has been given increased powers of delay, perhaps to one year, then the conflict of majority between the two houses would force them to come to an accommodation with one another if they wanted to pass the legislation in less than a year. Since the conflicting majorities would each reflect equally legitimate views within the public at large, this might be seen as an entirely appropriate situation in which checks and balances were actually working in practice. A similar argument could be made about a Seanad veto arising from a qualified majority.

The counter-argument is that not only is there a possibility of deadlock which could lead to a failure to pass urgently needed legislation but, if the deadlock were resolved by one house giving way, those voters who had supported the 'losing' majority in a popular election would then feel that the political system had offered them something and then snatched it away from them, and thereby become alienated and cynical.

Once more, when two houses are given real power yet represent different voices, which in a sense is the fundamental premise of bicameralism, then situations are almost bound to arise in which deadlock between the houses can only end with one prevailing over the other, and a consequent undervaluing of the voices represented in the 'losing' house. Once more, the attractiveness of this option depends upon a fundamental political decision about the extent to which confrontation between the two houses can be tolerated. We do feel, however, that the fact that majorities do not always get what they want is not an argument, in itself, against any form of direct election. If it was, direct elections might as well be abolished for many of the world's political institutions!

6 Conclusion

Each of the options outlined in the previous section has considerable merit, although introducing the more 'radical' changes will require, as we have seen, some fundamental political decisions. Our review of the ways in which the powers and functions of a future Seanad might interact does, however, enable us to make some general points in conclusion. In these we take into account both the comparative dimension and the history of Ireland's second chamber.

1. We feel that the case for the abolition of the Seanad has not been strongly enough made by its 'elite' critics, while there is clearly no groundswell of popular opinion in favour of abolishing the upper house. *Given the contribution that the current Seanad does in fact make, even if much of this is outside its 'core' role as a legislative chamber, we can see little to be gained by abolishing it.*

2. We also feel that the mainstream critique of the current Seanad carries considerable force. Having so little real power, and operating so much in the shadow of the Dáil and government, the Seanad is certainly not fulfilling the aspirations of the 1937 Constitution. Those who defined a role for the Seanad in 1937 anticipated neither the powerful government control of the legislature brought about by a combination of standing orders and the whip system, nor the arcane system of nominating and electing senators put into place by subsequent legislation. *This leads us to go along with the view that, while the Seanad should not be abolished it should indeed be reformed.*

3. Once we are in the business of reforming what in theory is one of the most important political institutions in the state, it scarcely seems worth fiddling around at the edges of the matter. *Thus we do not feel that there is a case for tinkering with the existing arcane legislation that defines the composition of the current Seanad, but rather for rewriting this from scratch to define the composition of a Seanad that will best equip it to make a real contribution to Irish political life in the twenty-first century.*

4. One issue to be addressed here is the extent to which the 1937 principle of vocational representation should be given a real, as opposed to a purely formal, role. We have reviewed the arguments for and against this in the main body of the paper. While the principle is very unusual in a comparative context, it does offer the possibility of bringing totally new voices into the Dáil, which will in turn have its own costs and benefits. *In our view, a thoroughgoing political discussion of the merits of vocationalism is worthwhile, and a case needs to be made for its retention as the primary basis of representation in the Seanad in the twenty-first century; of course, this issue is a quintessentially political matter.*

5. Comparative analysis has also drawn our attention to the unique right of the head of government to appoint members of the second chamber. In other countries, while the prime minister may have a role – indeed, possibly a determining voice – in such nominations, the formal appointments are made by the head of state. *We therefore suggest that consideration be given to transferring the right of appointment from the Taoiseach to the President, possibly with the requirement that the President act on the advice of the Taoiseach (though alternative arrangements for nominations could also be made).*

6. Existing provisions for university representation are both cumbersome and of questionable appropriateness. Most of those voting no longer have any connection, other than possibly one of sentiment, with the universities whose representatives they are choosing. *If university*

representation is to continue, therefore, methods should be devised to ensure that university senators represent their universities, rather than giving a special additional franchise to a large and disparate body of graduates most of whom have long departed from their colleges, and perhaps even from the country.

7   The first major issue to be confronted, therefore, is the social and political basis of the composition of a new Seanad. We have already pointed to some of the peculiar features of this body. It is important, however, also to recall the history of Seanad Éireann. This body came into existence as part of a formal agreement in 1922 between the new Irish government and representatives of southern unionists (though, of course, it might well have come into existence in any case even without this pressure). At least in its early years, it played an important representative role in reconciling this minority to life in independent Ireland. *There is therefore a case for looking carefully at the capacity of the Seanad to act as a voice for special groups that might otherwise be kept at a distance from Irish political life, such as representatives of the Irish abroad, of marginal groups within Irish society and, depending on certain very delicate constitutional and institutional matters that it would be dangerous to prejudge, of the two communities in Northern Ireland.*

8   The second major issue to be confronted is that of giving the Seanad new powers that do not overlap with those of the Dáil. These might include the review of senior public appointments or the conduct of tribunals of enquiry, as well as a number of others. The arguments in favour of doing this seem to us to be much stronger than the arguments against. The net result could well be an Irish political system that was more transparent and accountable, which almost everyone (at least almost everyone outside the core executive) would regard as a good thing. *We therefore suggest that very serious consideration indeed be given to the possibility of giving the Seanad new powers that do not overlap with those of the Dáil.*

9   The third major issue to be confronted is that of giving the Seanad new powers that would indeed overlap with those of the Dáil—that is, giving it enhanced power over the legislative process. This is intimately tied to the whole question of the legitimacy of the second chamber, and the issue of direct election. It seems to us that a radical shift to direct election is not merited unless the Seanad is also given enhanced powers in the legislative process. *Once more, we identify a fundamental issue that must be debated politically – the question whether it is desirable, whatever the situation in theory, to have a working system of checks and balances in the Irish legislative system, given the potential for conflict between the two houses of the legislature that such a system must inevitably imply.*

The present system in Ireland does not involve such conflict because the current Seanad has no teeth in what is a system of checks and balances in name only. But giving the Seanad teeth, of course, raises the possibility that it will sometimes bite.

Annexe 1: Data on 58 second houses of parliament, 1996

Chamber	State type	Characteristics of second chamber					Relative size of second chamber			
		power	size	selection process	term	min age	lower house size	ratio	population (000s)	ratio
Antigua and Barbuda Senate	unitary	less	17	A	5	21	19	89	65	4
Argentina Senate	federal	less	72	D	6b	30	257	28	34,182	475
Australia Senate	federal	less	76	D	6c	18	148	51	17,853	235
Austria Federal Council	federal	less	64	I	*	21	183	35	7,918	124
Bahamas Senate	unitary	less	16	A	5	30	49	33	272	17
Barbados Senate	unitary	less	21	A	5	30	28	75	261	12
Belgium Senate	federal	same	71	D 40 I 21 C 10		21	150	47	10,080	142
Belize Senate	unitary	less	8	A	5	18	29	28	210	26
Bolivia Senate	unitary	same	27	D	4	35	130	21	7,237	268
Bosnia and Herzegovina House of Peoples	federal	more	15	I	2	18	42	36	3,527	235
Brazil Senate	federal	same	81	D	8e	35	513	16	159,143	1,965
Burkina Faso House of Representatives	unitary	less	178	A	3	-	107	166	10,046	56
Canada Senate	federal	less	104	A	*	30	295	35	29,141	280
Chile Senate	unitary	same	46	D 38 A 8 E 0	8e	40	120	38	14,044	305
Colombia Senate	unitary	same	102	D	4	30	163	63	34,545	339
Congo Senate	unitary	less	60	I	6b	50	125	48	2,516	42
Croatia House of Counties	unitary	less	68	D 63 A 5	4	18	127	54	4,504	66
Dominican Republic Senate	unitary	same	30	D	4	25	120	25	7,684	256
Ethiopia Federal Council	federal	less	117	I	5	depends	550	21	53,435	457

95

Chamber	State type	Characteristics of second chamber					Relative size of second chamber			
		power	size	selection process	term	min age	lower house size	ratio	population (000s)	ratio
Fiji Senate	unitary	less	34	A	4	21	70	49	771	23
France Senate	unitary	less	321	I	9d	35	577	56	57,747	180
Germany Federal Council	federal	less	68	I	variable	18	672	10	81,278	1,195
Grenada Senate	unitary	less	13	A	5	18	15	87	92	7
Haiti Senate	unitary	less	27	D	6b	30	83	33	7,035	261
India Council of States	federal	less	245	I 233 A 12	6b	30	545	45	918,570	3,749
Ireland Senate	unitary	less	60	I 43 A 11 U 6	5	21	166	36	3,539	59
Italy Senate	unitary	same	326	D 315 A 9 E 2	5	40	630	52	57,157	175
Jamaica Senate	unitary	less	21	A	5	21	60	35	2,429	116
Japan House of Councillors	unitary	less	252	D	6c	21	500	50	124,815	495
Jordan Senate	unitary	more	40	A	4	40	80	50	5,198	130
Kazakstan Senate	unitary	less	47	I 40 A 7 E 0	4a	30	67	70	17,027	362
Kyrghyzstan Assembly of People's Reps.	unitary	less	70	D	5	25	35	200	4,667	67
Lesotho Senate	unitary	less	33	E 22 A 11	5	21	65	51	1,996	60
Malaysia Senate	federal	less	69	A 43 I 26	3	30	192	36	19,695	285
Mauritania Senate	unitary	less	56	I	6b	35	79	71	2,217	40
Mexico Senate	federal	same	128	D	6c	30	500	26	91,858	718
Namibia National Council	unitary	less	26	I	6	na	72	36	1,500	58
Nepal National Council	unitary	less	60	P 35 I 5 A 10	6b	35	205	29	21,360	356
Netherlands First Chamber	unitary	less	75	I	4	18	150	50	15,397	205
Pakistan Senate	federal	less	87	I 79 P 8	6c	30	217	40	136,645	1,571

96

Chamber	State type	Characteristics of second chamber					Relative size of second chamber			
		power	size	selection process	term	min age	lower house size	lower house ratio	population (000s)	population ratio
Palau Senate	unitary	less	14	D	4	25	16	88	17	1
Paraguay Senate	unitary	less	45	D	5	40	80	56	4,830	107
Philippines Senate	unitary	same	24	D	6c	35	250	10	66,188	2,758
Poland Senate	unitary	less	100	D	4	21	460	22	38,341	383
Romania Senate	unitary	less	143	D	4	35	341	42	22,922	160
Russian Federation Council of the Federation	federal	same	178	I	*	na	450	40	147,370	828
Saint Lucia Senate	unitary	less	11	A	5	21	18	61	141	13
South Africa Senate	unitary	less	90	I	5	18	400	23	40,555	451
Spain Senate	unitary	less	256	D 206 I 48	4	18	350	73	39,568	155
Swaziland Senate	unitary	same	30	A 20 I 10	5	18	65	46	832	28
Switzerland Council of States	federal	same	46	L		na	200	23	7,131	155
Thailand Senate	unitary	same	260	A	6	35	391	66	58,183	224
Trinidad and Tobago Senate	unitary	less	31	A	5	25	36	86	1,292	42
United Kingdom House of Lords	unitary	less	1,191	H 770 A 395 E 26		21	651	183	58,091	49
United States of America Senate	federal	more	100	D	6b	30	435	23	260,631	2,606
Uruguay Senate	unitary	same	31	D 30 E 1	5	30	99	31	3,167	102
Venezuela Senate	federal	same	49	D 46 E 1	5	30	201	24	21,378	436
Yugoslavia Chamber of Republics	federal	less	40	I	4	18	138	29	10,763	269

Notes: 'power of second chamber' is expressed in relation to the first chamber, as measured across a range of criteria; 'selection process': A-appointed; C-coopted; D-directly elected; E-ex officio; H-hereditary; I-indirectly elected; L-selected according to local arrangements (in practice, almost all directly elected); P-elected by members of the lower house; U-elected by university graduates. 'Term' refers to the term of office of senators; in certain cases elections are staggered: a-half retire every two years; b-one-third retire every two years; c-half retire every three years; d-one-third retire every three years, half retire every four years. The 'relative size' data refer respectively to the number of members in the lower house, the number of members of the upper house for each 100 members of the lower house, the population of the country in thousands and the population (in thousands) for each member of the second chamber

Sources: Inter-Parliamentary Union, 1996; CIA, 1995; United Nations, 1996; Derbyshire and Derbyshire, 1992; Europa, 1996; Keesing's, 1996; and other sources

Annexe 2: Relative power of west European second houses of parliament, 1980s

Country	Legislative domain		Executive domain	
	Competence	Power	Control	Independence
Unitary States				
Belgium*	high	high	high	low
France	high	medium	medium	high
Ireland	medium	low	low	low
Italy	high	high	high	low
Netherlands	low	high (low)	high (low)	low
Spain	high	low	medium	low
United Kingdom	medium	low	medium	high
*Denmark**	*high*	*high*	*high*	*high*
*Sweden**	*high*	*high*	*high*	*low*
Federal States				
Austria	low	low	low	high
Germany	low	medium	medium (low)	high
Switzerland	high	high	high	medium

Notes: The powers of the second chambers are defined as follows (where the three parameters in brackets refer respectively to the 'high', 'medium' and 'low' positions): **Competence**: type of legislation which the chamber may initiate or amend (all; all except a few; restricted to a few defined areas); **Power**: capacity of the chamber to veto legislation (absolute; limited or conditional; suspensive); **Control**: capacity of the chamber to appoint and dismiss the government and to review its work (appoint, dismiss and review; review only; limited right of review); **Independence**: capacity of the government to dissolve the chamber (none, but it *can* dissolve the lower house; none, it cannot dissolve either house; can dissolve both houses). Where two measures are given (one in brackets), the first refers to the constitutional or formal position, the one in brackets to the position in practice

*This refers to the position before the federalisation of Belgium. The positions of the Danish Landsting and the first chamber of the Swedish Riksdag before their abolition in 1953 and 1969 respectively have also been included

Source: adapted from information contained in Mastias and Grangé 1987: 19-37

Annexe 3: Political balance in selected first and second chambers, most recent election

Belgium	House (1995)	Senate (1995)
Socialist-PS	**21**	**11**
Socialist-SP	**20**	**9**
Christian Social-CVP	**29**	**12**
Christian Social-PSC	**12**	**7**
Liberal-VLD	21	10
Liberal-PRL	18	9
Greens-Ecolo	8	3
Greens-Agalev	5	2
Vlaams Blok	1	5
Volksunie	5	3
National Front	2	.
Total	150	71
Total, government	82	39
(percent)	(54.6)	(54.9)

Spain	House (1996)	Senate (1996)
People's Party	**156**	**133**
Socialist Workers' Party	141	96
United Left	21	.
Convergence and Unity	**16**	**11**
Basque Nationalist Party	**5**	**6**
Canarian Coalition	4	.
Galician Nationalist Party	2	.
Herri Batasuna	2	.
Others	3	10
Total	350	256
Total, government	177	150
(percent)	(50.6)	(58.6)

France*	House (1993)	Senate (1995)
RPR	**257**	**94**
UDF/Centrist Union	**215**	**59**
Socialists	57	75
Various right	23	.
Communists	23	15
Republicans/independents	.	46
Others	.	24
Unattached	25	8
Total	577	321
Total, government	472	153
(percent)	(81.8)	(47.7)

*refers to party groupings in parliament rather than to electoral parties

Netherlands	Second chamber (1994)	First chamber (1994)
Labour	**37**	**12**
Christian Democrats	34	19
Liberals	**21**	**23**
Democrats '66	**24**	7
Generation of the Elderly	7	2
Green Left	5	4
Others	12	4
Total	150	75
Total, government	92	44
(percent)	(61.3)	(58.7)

Switzerland	House (1995)	Council (1995)
Social Democrats	**54**	17
Radical Democrats	**45**	**5**
Christian Democrats	**34**	**16**
Swiss People's Party	**29**	**5**
Greens	9	.
Others	29	3
Total	200	46
Total, government	162	43
(percent)	(81.0)	(93.5)

Australia	House (1996)	Senate (1996)
Liberals	**75**	**21**
Labour	49	28
National Party	**18**	**6**
Others	6	11
Total	148	76
Total, government	93	27
(percent)	(62.8)	(35.5)

Canada	House (1993)	Senate (1996)
Liberal Party	**177**	**41**
Progressive Conservatives	2	58
Bloc Québecois	54	.
Reform Party	52	.
Others	9	5
Total	294	104
Total, government	177	41
(percent)	(60.2)	(39.4)

United Kingdom	Commons (1992)	Lords (1996)
Conservatives	**336**	**466**
Labour	271	111
Liberals	20	56
Crossbenchers	.	304
Others	24	108
Total	651	1,045
Total, government	336	466
(percent)	(51.6)	(44.6)

Note: Numbers reported are in some cases smaller than the full membership of the second chamber due to the omission of certain other categories of members. Parties in government are printed bold

Source: Inter-Parliamentary Union, 1996; Australia, 1996; Canada, 1996; United Kingdom, 1996

Annexe 4: Composition of Seanad Éireann, 1938-93

4a Distribution of senators by subpanel, 1938-93

Year	Nominating Bodies subpanel	Oireachtas subpanel
1938-44	21	22
1948	18	25
1951	17	26
1954-77	16	27
1981	18	25
1982	21	22
1983	21	22
1987	23	20
1989	24	19
1993	19	24

4b Distribution of panel senators by party, 1938-93

Year	Fianna Fáil	Fine Gael	Labour Party	Others
1938-1	25	14	1	3
1938-2	21	14	5	3
1943	21	13	7	2
1944	22	14	5	2
1948	17	14	7	5
1951	23	12	5	3
1954	19	12	7	5
1957	20	16	5	2
1961	23	11	7	2
1965	23	13	6	1
1969	20	17	5	1
1973	18	18	6	1
1977	20	18	5	0
1981	19	19	5	0
1982	20	18	5	0
1983	19	19	5	0
1987	24	16	3	0
1989	24	14	4	1
1993	19	16	5	3

Source: Coakley 1993; 1965 figure amended from *Irish Times*, 11 June 1965

REFERENCES

Ameller, Michel (1966), *Parliaments: a comparative study on the structure and functioning of representative institutions in fifty-five countries,* new edn, London: Cassell, for the Inter-Parliamentary Union

Australia: Senate (1996), *Australian Senate,* available HTTP: http://senate.aph.gov.au/ [1996, Nov 27]

Bagehot, Walter (1963), *The English Constitution,* [first published 1867] London: Fontana

Blondel, Jean (1973), *Comparative Legislatures,* Englewood Cliffs, NJ: Prentice-Hall

Bradshaw, Brendan (1973), 'The beginnings of modern Ireland', in Brian Farrell (ed), *The Irish Parliamentary Tradition,* Dublin: Gill and Macmillan, pp 70-87

Buckland, Patrick (1972), *Irish Unionism: one: the Anglo-Irish and the New Ireland 1885-1922,* Dublin: Gill and Macmillan

Canada: Parliament (1996), *Senators' biographies,* available HTTP: http://www.parl.gc.ca/ english/senate/bio-e/bio-e.htm [1996, Nov 27]

Carnarvon, Earl of, et al (1995), *Second Chamber: Some remarks on reforming the House of Lords,* London: Douglas Slater

Casey, James (1992), *Constitutional Law in Ireland,* 2nd edn, London: Sweet and Maxwell

Chubb, Basil (1970), *The Government and Politics of Ireland,* London: Oxford University Press

CIA (1996), CIA world factbook 1995, available HTTP: http://www.odci.gov/cia/publications /95fact/#r43 [1996, Nov 18]

Coakley, John (1980), 'The Irish senate election of 1977: voting in a small electorate', in *Parliamentary Affairs,* 33 (3), pp 322-331

Coakley, John (1987), 'The senate elections' in Brian Farrell and Howard Penniman (eds), *Ireland at the polls 1981, 1982 and 1987: a study of four general elections,* Washington, DC: American Enterprise Institute for Public Policy Research, pp 192-205

Coakley, John (1990), 'The elections to the senate' in Michael Gallagher and Richard Sinnott (eds), *How Ireland Voted 2: the general election of 1989,* Galway: PSAI Press, pp 148-161

Coakley, John (1993), 'The senate elections' in Michael Gallagher and Michael Laver (eds), *How Ireland Voted 3: the general election of 1992,* Dublin: Folens; Limerick: PSAI Press, pp 135-145

Commission on Vocational Organisation (1943), *Report*, Dublin: Stationery Office [chair: Most Rev Dr Michael Browne, Bishop of Galway]

Committee on the Constitution (1967), *Report of the Committee on the Constitution*, December 1967, Dublin: Stationery Office [chair: George Colley, TD]

Constitution Review Group (1996a), *Report of the Constitution Review Group*, Dublin: Stationery Office [chair: TK Whitaker]

Constitution Review Group (1996b), *Articles 15-27: 4: The National Parliament: Seanad Éireann* [unpublished discussion paper, May]

Dáil Éireann (1937), *Special report of the Special Committee on the Seanad Electoral (Panel Members), Bill, 1937: together with proceedings of the Special Committee,* Dublin: Stationery Office [chair: Eamon de Valera]

Derbyshire, J Denis and Derbyshire, Ian (1991), *World political systems: an introduction to comparative government,* New York: Chambers

Dooge, James (1987), 'The role of the Seanad', in Patrick Lynch and James Meenan (eds), *Essays in memory of Alexis FitzGerald,* Dublin: Incorporated Law Society of Ireland

Europa (1996), *The Europa World Yearbook 1996*, 2 vols, London: Europa Publications

France: Senate (1996), *Page de début du Sénat*, available HTTP: http://www.senat.fr/ [1996, Nov 18]

Gallagher, Michael (1993), *Irish elections 1922-44: results and analysis,* Limerick: PSAI Press

Garvin, Thomas (1969), *The Irish Senate,* Dublin: Institute of Public Administration

Government of Ireland (1996), *Revised Estimates for Public Services 1996,* Dublin: Stationery Office

Grangé, Jean (1987), 'Irlande: le Sénat (Seanad Éireann)', in Mastias and Grangé 1987, pp 291-316

Herman, Valentine with Françoise Mendel (1976), *Parliaments of the World: a reference compendium,* London: Macmillan

Inter-Parliamentary Union (1986), *Parliaments of the World: a comparative reference compendium,* 2 vols, Aldershot: Gower

Inter-Parliamentary Union (1996), *Parline Database*, available HTTP: http://www.ipu.org/ parline-e/parline.htm [1996, Oct 23]

Keesing's (1996), *Keesing's Record of World Events,* vol 42, 1996, Cambridge: Cartermill International

Kelly, JM (1994), *The Irish Constitution,* 3rd edn, edited by Gerard Hogan and Gerry Whyte, Dublin: Butterworths

Köhn, Leo, (1932), *The Constitution of the Irish Free State,* London: George Allen and Unwin

Kristan, Ivan (1996), *Bicameralism of the Slovene Parliament,* paper presented to the third regional conference of the central European political science associations, Bled, 22-23 November

Laundy, Philip (1989), *Parliaments in the Modern World,* Aldershot: Dartmouth

Manning, Maurice (1970), *The Blueshirts,* Dublin: Gill and Macmillan

Manning, Maurice (1978), 'The senate election', in Howard L Penniman (ed), *Ireland at the Polls: the* Dáil *election of 1977,* Washington, DC: American Enterprise Institute for Public Policy Research, pp 165-73

Marongiu, Antonio (1968), *Medieval Parliaments: a comparative study,* SJ Woolf (trans), London: Eyre and Spottiswoode

Mastias, Jean and Jean Grangé (eds) (1987), *Les Secondes Chambres du Parlement en Europe Occidentale,* Paris: Economica

Mill, John Stuart (1912), 'Considerations on representative government' in *On liberty. Representative government. The subject of women. Three essays,* London: Oxford University Press, pp 145-423 [originally published 1861]

Morgan, David Gwynn (1990), *Constitutional Law of Ireland,* 2nd edn, Dublin: Round Hall Press

Myers, AR (1975), *Parliaments and estates in Europe to 1789,* London: Thames and Hudson

Norton, Philip (1990), 'General introduction', in Philip Norton (ed), *Legislatures,* Oxford: Oxford University Press, pp 1-16

O'Sullivan, Donal (1940), *The Irish Free State and its Senate: a study in contemporary politics,* London: Faber and Faber

Oireachtas Éireann (1928), *Report of the Joint Committee on the constitution of Seanad Éireann, together with proceedings of the Joint Committee,* Dublin: Stationery Office [chair: Michael Hayes]

Oireachtas Éireann (1947), *Report of the Joint Committee on Seanad Panel Elections,* Dublin: Stationery Office [chair: Frank Fahy]

Paxton, John (1975), *World Legislatures*, London: Macmillan

Seanad Éireann (1953), *Report of the Select Committee on the Seanad Éireann (Panel Members), Bill, 1952, together with the proceedings of the Select Committee,* Dublin: Stationery Office [chair: Liam Ó Buachalla]

Seanad Éireann (1993), *Seanad General Election February 1993,* Dublin: Stationery Office

Seanad Electoral Law Commission (1959), *Report,* Dublin: Stationery Office [chair: Joseph A McCarthy, SC]

Second House of the Oireachtas Commission (1936), *Report,* Dublin: Stationery Office [chair: Hugh Kennedy]

Slovenia: National Council (1996), *National Council home page,* available HTTP: http://www.sigov.si/cgi-bin/spl/dsvet/ang/welcome.htm ?language=winee [1996, Dec 2]

Smyth, John MacG (1972), *The Theory and Practice of the Irish Senate,* Dublin: Institute of Public Administration

Uluots, J and J Klesment (eds) (1937), *Die Verfassung der Republik Estland,* Tallinn: Estländische Druckerei

United Kingdom: House of Lords (1996), *Information about the House of Lords,* http://www.parliament.the-stationery-office.co.uk/pa/ld/ldhome.htm [1996, Nov 26]

United Nations (1996), Department for Economic and Social Information and Policy Analysis: Population Division, *Population Information Network,* available GOPHER: gopher://gopher.undp.org:70/00/ungophers/popin/wdtrends/pop1994 [1996, Nov 4]

University of Hamburg (1996), *International Constitutional Law Project* [texts of contemporary constitutions], available HTTP: http://www.law.cornell.edu/law/ [1996, Nov 18]

Wheare, KC (1968), *Legislatures,* 2nd ed, London: Oxford University Press

Appendix III

Annexes 21-23, from *Report of the Committee on the Constitution* (1967)

ANNEX 21

Number of former Deputies elected to the Seanad

Year	number elected	percentage
1938 (1)	17	35
1938 (2)	19	39
1943	16	33
1944	14	29
1948	14	29
1951	15	31
1954	13	26
1957	17	35
1961	13	26
1965	12	25
1969	7	14
1973	7	14
1977	12	24
1981	8	16
1982	10	20
1983	11	22
1987	8	16
1989	14	29
1993	16	33

ANNEX 21 (A)

Number of former Deputies nominated by the Taoiseach to the Seanad

Year	% of members nominated	% of 11 nominees
1969	3	27
1973	1	9
1977	0	–
1981	0	–
1982	2	18
1983	1	9
1987	2	18
1989	4	36
1993	3	27

ANNEX 22

Bills amended by the Seanad

Year	Bills passed without amendment	with amendments	amendments agreed to by Dáil	certain amendments agreed to and others not agreed to by Dáil	certain amendments agreed to, others agreed to as amended and/or consequential amendments made by Dáil
1938	15	2	2	–	–
1939	20	8	8	–	–
1940	23	6	5	–	1
1941	16	7	6	–	1
1942	12	9	8	–	1
1943	13	5	4	–	1
1944	10	6	6	–	–
1945	21	11	10	–	1
1946	14	13	11	–	2
1947	30	7	7	–	–
1948	18	–	–	–	–
1949	19	3	3	–	–
1950	21	3	2	1	–
1951	14	3	3	–	–
1952	16	5	5	–	–
1953	19	4	4	–	–
1954	20	4	4	–	–
1955	20	3	3	–	–
1956	25	8	8	–	–
1957	16	6	5	1	–
1958	25	3	3	–	–
1959	25	5	5	–	–
1960	24	7	6	–	1
1961	30	7	7	–	–
1962	20	6	6	–	–
1963	18	5	5	–	–
1964	17	4	4	–	–
1965	14	4	3	–	1
1966	20	5	5	–	–

/continued

Year	Bills passed without amendment	with amendments	amendments agreed to by Dáil	certain amendments agreed to and others not agreed to by Dáil	certain amendments agreed to, others agreed to as amended and/or consequential amendments made by Dáil
1967	12	5	3	1	2
1968	16	11	4	–	–
1969	20	–	–	–	–
1970	14	6	5	–	1
1971	16	4	4	–	–
1972	22	5	4	–	–
1973	21	3	3	–	–
1974	23	2	2	–	–
1975	16	2	1	1	–
1976	23	3	3	–	–
1977	21	5	5	–	–
1978	21	7	5	–	–
1979	33	3	3	–	–
1980	33	2	2	–	–
1981	25	2	2	–	–
1982	22	1	–	–	–
1983	31	1	–	–	–
1984	21	2	–	–	1
1985	17	2	2	–	–
1986	22	2	2	–	–
1987	23	1	1	–	1
1988	19	2	1	–	–
1989	15	1	1	–	–
1990	26	2	3	–	–
1991	19	5	5	–	–
1992	23	5	5	–	–
1993	27	3	2	–	1
1994	19	8	8	–	–
1995 up to 19 September	14	4	2	1	1

ANNEX 23

Money Bills on which Seanad made recommendations

Year	Money Bills accepted without recommendations	with recommendations	recommendations accepted by Dáil	recommendations rejected by Dáil	Bill amended by Dáil in consequence of acceptance of recommendations
1938	11	–	–	–	–
1939	8	–	–	–	–
1940	6	–	–	–	–
1941	5	1	–	–	1
1942	6	–	–	–	–
1943	6	–	–	–	–
1944	6	–	–	–	–
1945	6	–	–	–	–
1946	9	1	1	–	–
1947	12	1	–	1	–
1948	6	–	–	–	–
1949	9	–	–	–	–
1950	7	–	–	–	–
1951	11	1	1	–	1
1952	8	–	–	–	–
1953	13	–	–	–	–
1954	13	–	–	–	–
1955	6	–	–	–	–
1956	13	–	–	–	–
1957	10	–	–	–	–
1958	6	–	–	–	–
1959	12	–	–	–	–
1960	15	–	–	–	–
1961	10	–	–	–	–
1962	12	–	–	–	–
1963	11	–	–	–	–
1964	17	–	–	–	–
1965	7	–	–	–	–
1966	3	–	–	–	–

/continued

Year	Money Bills accepted without recommendations	with recommendations	recommendations accepted by Dáil	recommendations rejected by Dáil	Bill amended by Dáil in consequence of acceptance of recommendations
1967	4	–	–	–	–
1968	12	–	–	–	–
1969	12	–	–	–	–
1970	5	–	–	–	–
1971	7	–	–	–	–
1972	6	1	1	–	1
1973	8	–	–	–	–
1974	9	1	1	–	1
1975	9	1	1	–	1
1976	9	–	–	–	–
1977	9	–	–	–	–
1978	7	–	–	–	–
1979	5	1	1	–	1
1980	7	–	–	–	–
1981	7	–	–	–	–
1982	5	–	–	–	–
1983	9	–	–	–	–
1984	5	–	–	–	–
1985	3	–	–	–	–
1986	6	–	–	–	–
1987	7	–	–	–	–
1988	5	–	–	–	–
1989	3	–	–	–	–
1990	3	–	–	–	–
1991	3	–	–	–	–
1992	4	–	–	–	–
1993	4	–	–	–	–
1994	4	–	–	–	–
1995 up to 19 September	nil				

List of Submissions

Daisy Corrigan

Fianna Fáil group of senators

Dr Garret FitzGerald

Senator Tom Fitzgerald

Justin Keating

Alderman Seán Dublin Bay Rockall Loftus

Brian McCarthy

Senator Jarlath McDonagh

Michael McKeown

John A Murphy

Senator David Norris

Conor Cruise O'Brien

Donal Ó Brolcháin

John O'Connell

Fergus O'Donovan

John Robb

Brian Shanley

Trevor T West

T K Whitaker

Senator G V Wright

Index

Note: page numbers in italics refer to the text of Bunreacht na hÉireann given passim *in the left-hand margins)*

report on Seanad Éireann 15-31

    composition 19

    continuance of 18

    functions 18-19

    functional and vocational representation 19-20

    general election 21

    MEPs and Northern Ireland representation 20

    parliamentary questions 20

    participation of ministers in debates 20

    polling day 21

    postal ballot 21

    redundant Article 22

    requirement of citizenship 21

    resignation of Taoiseach's nominees 21

CORK REGIONAL TECHNICAL COLLEGE 11

COLOMBIA 39, 95

CONGO 41, 95

CONNOLLY, JOSEPH 64

COSGRAVE, W T 54

COUNCIL OF STATE *6, 7, 8, 9, 11,* 63

CROATIA 35, 41, 42, 95

CZECH REPUBLIC 15, 36

DENMARK 15, 25, 36, 69, 88, 99

DE VALERA, EAMON 4, 54, 64

DISABLED PEOPLE
representation in the Seanad 23, 24

DOMINICAN REPUBLIC 39, 95

DOOGE, JAMES 5, 64

DUBLIN CITY UNIVERSITY 11

EMIGRANTS
representation in the Seanad 18, 24, 68, 75

ESRI
Poverty, income and welfare in Ireland 23

ESSAYS IN THE MEMORY OF ALEXIS FITZGERALD 5

ESTONIA 15, 43

ETHIOPIA 35, 41, 95

EUROPEAN PARLIAMENT 7, 10, 20
elections to 23, 65, 76

EUROPEAN UNION 6, 35
legislation of 8-9
MEPs 8, 10
policies of 9

FIJI 42, 96

FINLAND 15, 25, 36, 69

FRANCE 3, 4, 15, 25, 27, 30, 36, 40, 41, 44, 63, 96, 99, 101

GENDER
equality 24
imbalance 7-8

GERMANY 25, 27, 33, 35, 40, 41, 46, 50, 96, 99

GLENAVY, LORD 54

GREAT BRITAIN. *See Britain*

GREECE 69

GRENADA 37, 42, 96

HAITI 40, 96

HIGHER EDUCATION AUTHORITY 11

HOUSEHOLD BUDGET SURVEY 23

HUNGARY 15

INTER-PARLIAMENTARY UNION
database of 4, 33, 36, 37, 98, 102

IRISH FREE STATE 5, 53, 54. *See also*
Saorstát Éireann
Constitution of 4, 40, 64, 67, 79, 89, 93
Senate of 5, 44, 54
   abolition of 4, 16, 55

ICELAND 15, 25, 69

INDIA 35, 42, 96

ITALY 15, 25, 27, 40, 42, 43, 44, 49, 50, 56,
96, 99

JAMAICA 42, 96

JAPAN 35, 39, 96

JEFFERSON, THOMAS 5

JOHNSON, THOMAS 67

JORDAN 42, 96

KAZAKHSTAN 42, 44, 96

KENNEDY, HUGH 65

KYRGHYZSTAN 35, 39, 48, 96

LATVIA 15

LAVER, MICHAEL 3, 5, 6, 11, 25, 32, 65

LESOTHO 42, 43, 96

LETTERKENNY REGIONAL
TECHNICAL COLLEGE 11

LIMERICK REGIONAL TECHNICAL
COLLEGE 11

LITHUANIA 15

LUXEMBOURG 15, 25, 35

LYNCH, DR KATHLEEN 19, 23, 68

MACDERMOT, FRANK 66

MALAYSIA 42, 45. 96

MAURITANIA 41, 96

MAYNOOTH, ST PATRICK'S COLLEGE
11

MCCARTHY, JOSEPH 17

MEPs 8, 10, 20, 24, 27, 29

MEXICO 40, 96

MICRONESIA
Federated States of 37

MONEY BILLS *5, 6, 8,* 16

MOYLAN, SEAN 64

NAMIBIA 35, 41, 96

NATIONAL COUNCIL FOR EDUCATION
AWARDS 11

NATIONAL ECONOMIC AND SOCIAL
FORUM (NESF) 6, 24